STEVIE WONDER

JOHN SWENSON

PERENNIAL LIBRARY

Harper & Row, Publishers, New York
Cambridge, Philadelphia, San Francisco, Washington
London, Mexico City, São Paulo, Singapore, Sydney

Photographs: Page 1: *Stevie Wonder in 1969, at the time of the release of his album "For Once In My Life." Page 4/5: Little Stevie Wonder blowing up a storm with some Parisian contemporaries. During his 1963 French tour, Stevie was presented with a gold harmonica by boys representing each of the districts of Paris.*

STEVIE WONDER. Text copyright © 1986 by John Swenson. All rights reserved. Printed in the United States of America. No part of this book may be used or reproduced in any manner whatsoever without written permission except in the case of brief quotations embodied in critical articles and reviews. For information address Harper & Row, Publishers, Inc., 10 East 53rd Street, New York, N.Y. 10022.

FIRST U.S. EDITION

First published in Great Britain by Plexus Publishing Limited.

Cover and book design by Ken Kitchen.

LIBRARY OF CONGRESS CATALOG CARD NUMBER: 86-45167

ISBN: 0-06-097067-7

86 87 88 89 90 MPC 10 9 8 7 6 5 4 3 2 1

CONTENTS

Preface

It is not hard to imagine why Stevie Wonder poses unique difficulties as the subject for a biographer. Stevie's delight in practical joking and Motown Records' careful exploitation of his career have combined to shroud his personal history in quasi-myths. Because he is blind, Stevie Wonder's movements are of course somewhat restricted, and because he has been signed to Motown Records since childhood, his public life and biographical details have been carefully manipulated from the outset. So well manipulated, in fact, that it is possible, though certainly unlikely, that virtually everything known about Stevie Wonder (or any other Motown artist) is a carefully constructed piece of fiction assembled by Motown press agents. It is far more likely that some of the details of his life are doctored bits of mythology that deviate only far enough from the truth to fit Motown's purposes.

Stevie Wonder has been very carefully guarded; by his mother, by his brothers, who virtually run his business, and by Motown, the most secretive, close-mouthed record company in operation. Those interests have attempted to paint him as a demi-god, a miracle straight from heaven onto your turntable.

I have, accordingly, used as much skepticism as could reasonably be applied to the information culled from a variety of sources, including Stevie's own comments about his life. In my own interviews with him it occurred to me that the details of his personal life are of little specific interest to him in a historic sense. Although he knows who a particular love song is written about it does not concern him if the public does not know it. He originally wrote *My Cherie Amour*, for example, as "Oh My Marsha". In private conversation, Wonder seems more concerned with larger, philosophical and religious issues. And because of his sense of humor, it is conceivable that some of his statements about his past are meant as put-ons, his private lampoons of the star-making process. He also has an acute sense of humor in response to personal questions, like the time he told *Jet* magazine that he wanted to be the judge of a beauty contest.

Nevertheless, it is impossible to think of him as duplicitous once you have met him. The way he shakes your hand, ignoring glib public relations surfaces, the manner in which he aims conversation intently at his interlocutor yet talks in cosmic abstractions as if he is trying to explain a complex philosophical theory every time he addresses an idea; these are the gestures of a man whose sincerity is beyond question.

Talking to Stevie Wonder is an eerie kind of exchange. He is so attuned to sightless perception that you keep thinking he can see every damn thing that is there. He walks into someone's living room for the interview, nods a bit in different directions and with a delighted twist of his massive neck exclaims "Wow, really nice place you got here." It is so convincing an assertion that you find yourself looking around the room to see what you missed.

So really you have to take some of what Stevie says with a grain of salt, but you can be sure that he is not pulling punches when he talks about his passions – playing music, speaking up about the way politics interacts badly with human interests, or those hard-to-pin-down epistemological questions that are the basis of all religion and philosophy. People have belittled Wonder for tackling such subjects in celebrity interviews, but he deserves a lot of credit for speaking his mind on sensitive issues. "Being physically blind is no crime," he says, "but being spiritually blind is a serious handicap."

1. Second Sight

It was a Saturday, the day before Mother's Day, 13 May, 1950. Though it was officially spring, the slate black sky over Saginaw threatened rain and the bitter cold wind sliced across Lake Huron and the Michigan peninsula, bringing frosty reminders of the desolate winter that refused to die.

Lula Mae Hardaway grimaced with pain. Her ashen gray face strained in unison with her abdomen as she pushed with all her might at the warm, wet baby struggling to the mouth of its cave. The hospital bed was damp with the sweat of Lula's labor, but despite her pain, giving birth brought Lula a deep religious joy, and she worked herself into a semi-delirious trance as her body produced its creation.

When the baby was completely born, Lula felt angels' wings soothe her aching body. Dimly, she watched as her child, the umbilical cord cut and tied, was hoisted away. The first cry brought a smile to her lips. It was a boy, her third, and his cry was strong and healthy, his first song. Lula's baby sang the song of his life. She would call him Steveland.

Lula had been worried when the labor started a month too soon. Birth defects were common in the ghettos of Saginaw, a bleak and extremely poor town whose only claim to fame was that it had the world's purest water. Geographically, Saginaw is well within the Canadian latitudes and the climate is exceedingly hostile. Once it had been a boom town, the cornerstone of the "green gold" logging boom of the 1880s, and the rich mineral deposits of Northern Michigan made it an important mining center. But for the poor, and especially for the Negroes who migrated north to fill jobs created by industrial expansion, there was no real recovery from the Great Depression of the 1930s. Winter was a killing season, and with the epidemics of respiratory diseases that ravaged the city, pregnancy was a dangerous physical condition.

On this 13 May, the front page of the *Saginaw News* editorialized a bitter protest against Re-publican budget cuts that jeopardized the state government's ability to meet its social program needs. Another front page article warned of a full-scale Southern filibuster in Congress to stop an important piece of civil rights legislation sponsored by the Illinois Democrat, Senator Lucas. Banner headlines in the sports section declared "A Victory" as the American Bowling Congress voted to do away with its long-standing policy of limiting membership to "white males only". The Detroit Tigers, the closest major league baseball team, had moved into first place in the American League after taking a double-header from the Boston Red Sox. The *Michigan* movie theater was showing a double feature: *The Story of Seabiscuit* starring Shirley Temple and *Davy Crockett, Indian Scout* starring George Montgomery.

Meanwhile, the infant Steveland Morris was being placed in an incubator in the special care baby unit — a normal medical procedure for a baby born prematurely. Though he was not technically blind at the moment of his birth, by the time Steveland was removed from the incubator he was sightless. The reason for his blindness is still subject to speculation: "I have a dislocated nerve in one eye," he later explained, "and a cataract on the other. It may have happened from being in the incubator too long and receiving too much oxygen." Steve is now aware of the dilemma facing doctors in those days, working in underfunded public hospitals fighting to save the lives of the most disadvantaged. "A girl who was born that same day I was was also put into the incubator, and she died," he said, "I personally think I'm lucky to be alive."

Whatever the reason for it, the boy who would become Stevie Wonder was born at the margin of American society with an affliction that could well have amounted to a death sentence, but because his mother was a strong, courageous woman he was saved from the fate often suffered by the weak in the poverty-stricken black communities of the time. Lula, and women like her, provided most of what little stability existed in them. Her life was typical of the miserable conditions suffered by the economically downtrodden in the industrial north. Women were commonly heads of households when adult males, unable to find work to make ends meet and stranded in a strange city, reacted to the extra economic burden of children by running away from home and the responsibilities they could not meet. Welfare rules which made state economic aid available to husbandless women with children provided another contributing factor to the breakdown of the family structure (in Stevie's childhood school district 50 per cent of the students were from families with only one parent).

Steve's actual surname, the name of his natural father which he would later use on some songwriting credits, was Judkins, although the last name on his birth certificate was Morris. His two older half-brothers, Calvin and Milton, were Hardaways. Either way, neither of the fathers lived in the home. Stevie answers questions about confusion surrounding his name by saying: "I have a lovely mother and she was fortunate enough to be married to more than one man." Lula did the best she could to feed and clothe her three children, supplementing the meager public assistance she received from the state by working as a cleaning lady in private homes.

Stevie has no distinct memories of his life in Saginaw, though he does recall that it was cold. "There's one thing I always laugh about," he later said, "when I think back to when we were little kids in Saginaw. My father used to tell us that Saginaw was only twelve miles from the North Pole, and me and my stepbrother Calvin used to go around telling people that we were born twelve miles from the North Pole. I believed that for a long time."

In 1953 Lula moved the family downstate to the teeming city of Detroit in search of better living conditions. The family's lot improved, if only in escaping the impossibly bleak Saginaw winters. They moved into a shabby but relatively comfortable slum dwelling in the east side black ghetto. Over the next few years the family's stability improved considerably. Lula got back together with Paul Hardaway, the father of her first two boys, and bore three more of his children, Larry, Timothy and Steve's only sister, Renee. Paul established himself in a bagel bakery and the Hardaways began to eke out a slightly better living.

Lula took particular care of her blind boy and prayed to God that his sight be restored. She consulted public welfare doctors, quacks and faith healers for help, but while some made extravagant claims, none could effect a cure. "They talked that stuff," says Steve, a little bitterly, "but they are crazy, man. They can't wake up the dead. There were things that they said they could do, but I went to doctors that said 'if there was any way that we could do it we would definitely try'."

Lula's strong Baptist faith and rudimentary understanding of the Bible convinced her that her son's blindness was not without purpose. "I always wanted a musician in my family," she says, "so God blessed me with Steve. And I didn't know that He would take his eyesight for the gift, for music. It really did hurt me. But God have blessed me. He have blessed Steve. He have blessed the whole family and I'm really happy."

Though it was hard on her, God willed her a child who was "different" and she acted accordingly. Lula believed that blind children were a little closer to God and she knew about the tradition of "second sight" in the black community. Indeed, sightless people have been honored as magicians, priests and oracles throughout history. It was generally held that music was the best medium within which to express second sight, and it was also one of the very few things a blind black man could do to support himself. Many of the country blues performers who traveled the south, accompanying their singing with crude, forceful guitar playing, were blind or otherwise handicapped, and a few of them made extraordinary impressions on American music. Blind Lemon Jefferson, a Texas bluesman who was one of the bestselling recording artists of the 1920s, brought country blues to the pinnacle of its creativity and influence with the stirring rhythms and audacious conception of his playing. Jefferson's influence was felt in every corner of the blues world, from T-Bone Walker in Texas to the urban blues of Muddy Waters in Chicago and John Lee Hooker in Detroit. Jefferson himself froze to death in a Chicago tenement in 1930.

Lula had no musical instruments to give Steveland, but she had other ways of encourag-

Right: Stevie in Central Park, New York City in the early sixties. Like most blind people, Stevie Wonder found his other senses were particularly acute, and he has never let his blindness interfere with his enjoyment of life.

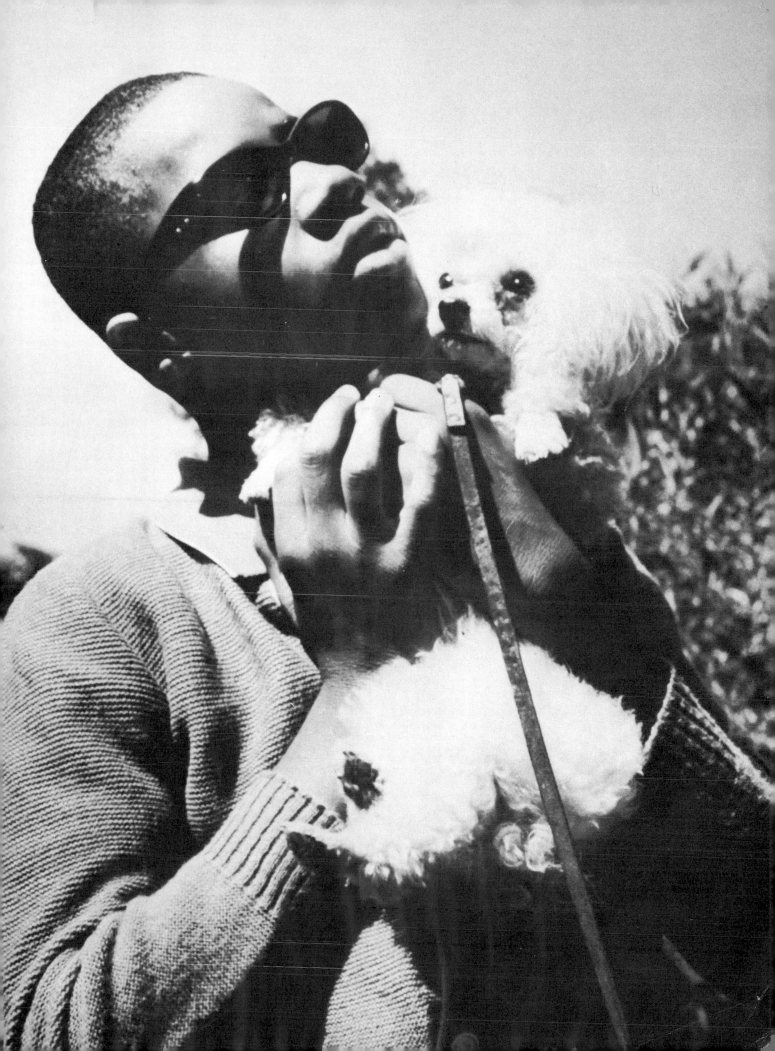

ing him in that direction. His musical education began by listening to the radio. "Sundown", a blues and R&B program broadcast from the local radio station WCHB, was his favorite show. His first musical recollections date from the mid-fifties. The first song he remembers hearing was *Pledging My Love* by Johnny Ace, a blues singer who killed himself playing Russian Roulette on Christmas Eve in 1954.

Stevie listened with amazement to the music of B. B. King, Little Walter, Bill Doggett, Jimmy Reed, Bobby Bland, Jackie Wilson, the Coasters, Chuck Willis, LaVerne Baker and others: "For the most part, music was something inside of me," he said. "I'd listen to TV and radio, and I'd sing around the house, but no one put any emphasis on it. I didn't, especially, because I was shy. I spent a lot of time listening to the radio, and I was able to relate to the different instruments and know what they were. I began to know them by name."

He began to develop an extraordinary auditory perception which family and friends delighted in testing. People would throw money down on the table and ask, "What's that, Stevie?" He was a master at this game. "That's a dime," he'd answer . . . "That's a quarter" . . . "That's a nickle." The only time they could stump him was on the difference between a penny and a nickle.

The loss of one sense tends to enhance the other senses since they play a larger role in establishing the person's awareness of reality, and Steve's sense of hearing was almost unnaturally acute. "There's one thing you've got to remember," he says. "Sound happens all the time. If you put your hands right up to your ears, if you close your eyes and move your hands back and forth, you can hear the sound getting closer and farther away. Sound bounces off everything, there's always something happening."

To some extent, Steve's sonar helped him to keep up with the neighborhood kids, enabling him to do some pretty amazing things: "I did the normal things, swimming, skating, playing army, fighting. I used to hop barns with all the other dudes. You know those small sheds they used to have in the back of houses? In the ghetto where I lived, we'd hop atop them from one to the other. I remember one time my aunt came in and said 'OK Steve, Mama said don't be doin' that,' and I said 'Aw, fuck you,' and there's some neighbors out and they said 'Aw, child, you oughta' be

Stevie checks out the law. In his early years at Motown everyone was the butt of his constant practical joking.

ashamed of yourself, I thought you was a child of the Lord, you out there cussin' 'n' everything.'" This all happened in the back alley behind the house. Stevie ignored the scolding, continuing to jump from shed to shed. His last jump landed him in his mother's arms, though, and he was punished with an ironing cord whipping.

Being blind was not going to stop Steve from being precocious, and he gave his mother cause to use the ironing cord on more than one occasion. In fact, he recalls becoming first aware of his blindness by getting in trouble. "I guess that I first became aware that I was blind — and I

just vaguely remember this — when I'd be wallowing around in the back of the house on the grass, and I kept getting into the dog manure, and my mother would get on me about that. She explained that I couldn't move about so much, that I'd have to try and stay in one place. I never really wondered much about my blindness or asked questions about it, because to me, really, being blind was normal; since I had never seen it wasn't abnormal for me. But I know it used to worry my mother and I know she prayed for me to have sight some day, so I finally just told her that I was *happy* being blind, and I thought it was a gift from God, and I think she felt better after that."

Stevie's adjustment to his condition has never been hampered by an unwillingness to accept his handicap. Since he was a child, Stevie began testing the outside world, almost daring it to prevent him from doing things that sighted people could do. Though he lived an understandably sheltered social life as a child, he had a keen sense of adventure and curiosity that kept him trying to relate to other people around him. These traits developed as he grew older and people who have met Steve as an adult are

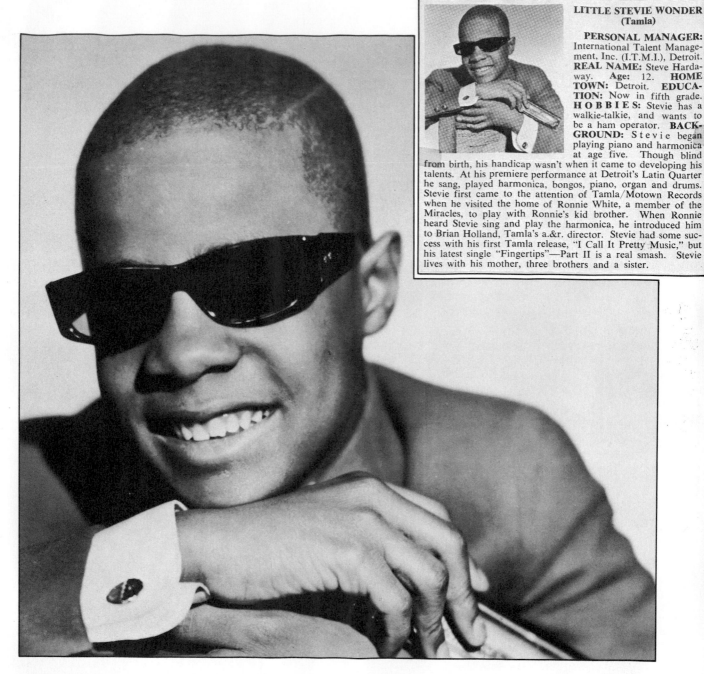

LITTLE STEVIE WONDER
(Tamla)

PERSONAL MANAGER: International Talent Management, Inc. (I.T.M.I.), Detroit. **REAL NAME:** Steve Hardaway. **Age:** 12. **HOME TOWN:** Detroit. **EDUCATION:** Now in fifth grade. **HOBBIES:** Stevie has a walkie-talkie, and wants to be a ham operator. **BACKGROUND:** Stevie began playing piano and harmonica at age five. Though blind from birth, his handicap wasn't when it came to developing his talents. At his premiere performance at Detroit's Latin Quarter he sang, played harmonica, bongos, piano, organ and drums. Stevie first came to the attention of Tamla/Motown Records when he visited the home of Ronnie White, a member of the Miracles, to play with Ronnie's kid brother. When Ronnie heard Stevie sing and play the harmonica, he introduced him to Brian Holland, Tamla's a.&r. director. Stevie had some success with his first Tamla release, "I Call It Pretty Music," but his latest single "Fingertips"—Part II is a real smash. Stevie lives with his mother, three brothers and a sister.

amazed by the fact that he roller-skates, swims, goes bowling, counts himself a champion air hockey player and has a passion for going to the movies.

Stevie also had a keen sense of wit even as a child, and would get involved in some wild exchanges with his sighted siblings. Once Lula left Stevie in the care of his older brothers Milton and Calvin, who related to his blindness in a pretty comical way. "Stevie needs some more light," they joked. "Wonder what we can do to get him some more light?" They tossed lit matches in the garbage can to make enough light for their blind brother to see and, according to Stevie, almost burned the house down with the ensuing bonfire.

Sex was another source of mischief for the young Stevie. "We listened to Redd Foxx and did all that stuff!" he boasts. "We tried to sneak and do it to little girls. As a matter of fact I got in more trouble than some of the sighted cats. I used to sneak girlfriends up to the railroad tracks."

Though Stevie's childhood recollections are

Above: *Stevie's publicity shot and (inset) press details issued in 1963 when* Fingertips Part 2 *reached Number One in the US. Stevie was actually thirteen years old, but it served Motown's purpose to make him appear younger.*

mostly on the lighter side, he faced his share of fear and loneliness as well, emotions which would later surface in his songwriting. It was at least until he was nine before he was ever able to go out by himself because he would always have a sighted chaperone with him, so he was rarely placed in situations where he'd be scared or made to feel alone. He does recall one frightening episode with his natural father, however. "This was after he and my mother had broken up – I must have been around seven or eight – he said to me, 'You want to go, Steve, with me? We gonna go get some candy and stuff, bubble gum and stuff . . . ride the bus . . .' I was jumping up and down and was excited about it, and we went over to his house and he had a piano and a saxophone. I stayed there for a while . . . and then one day I remember him having to go off somewhere and he stayed away for a long time and left me alone. That was the first time I got upset and I started to cry about that. But after a while I just said, hey, forget it, and I just went on to sleep. I was just afraid because the surroundings weren't familiar to me."

Steve was also aware as a child of the hardships his family faced because of its economic status. "I would love to do a TV special that would tell many things people don't know about me – like how when I was younger my mother, my brothers and I had to go on the dry dock where there was coal and steal some to keep warm. To a poor person that is not stealing, that is not crime; it's a necessity."

The first musical instruments Stevie encountered were crude percussion pieces, cans filled with rocks or marbles, pots and pans beaten with spoons or sticks. "I was always hittin' things," he says, "like beating on tables with a spoon, or beating these little cardboard drums they used to give kids. I'd beat 'em to death."

Every year for Christmas Steve would get a toy drum set, but the fragile skins would quickly break under the non-stop barrage he gave them. "The first time I really felt the power of music," he recalls, "was on a family picnic at Belle Island, a lake park in Detroit. Someone had hired a band, and I sat on the drummer's lap.

"He let me play the drums. It was a thrill I'll never forget. People applauded and one man gave me three quarters. Man, I felt like I had a fortune in my pocket. Later, when I'd sing or play for fun at functions, people would give me dollars, but I'd never take them. I just wanted quarters. Paper money doesn't jingle."

One Christmas, the Lion's Club, a neighborhood social organization, held a party for blind kids and gave Steve his first proper drum kit. Unfamiliar with how it was supposed to look, he began playing the drums upside down with the metal snares stretched across the skin facing him. When they told him to turn it over he protested, saying he liked it that way.

Steve had an innate flair for the drums, but occasionally he also had the chance to play a next-door neighbor's piano. The woman who owned the piano left it with Steve when she moved away. "I was about seven," he says, "still so small I could barely reach the pedals. I liked to play with the keys. I kept asking 'When they gonna bring the piano over, Momma?' I never realized how important that was going to be to me."

However, during his early childhood it was the harmonica which became the instrument that Steve was most familiar with, and the one that would be crucial to his eventual discovery: "When I was very little, a friend of the family's who was also a barber – I remember his name was Laud – gave me a harmonica. It was a charm off his key-ring. I became the leader of the harmonica band at school. With music, I belonged."

Every night Steve listened to the "Sundown" show on radio and tried to mimic harmonica and saxophone parts he heard in songs with his tiny instrument. "I started playing the blues. Jimmy Reed's blues, Bobby 'Blue' Bland's. I used to sit by my radio and listen. Took a little of everybody's style and made up my own."

Eventually Steve got a Hohner chromatic harmonica as a gift from an uncle. "The second harmonica was more expressive," he says. "It had more complexity and a different style than the toy harmonica." The youngster's phenomenal ear enabled him to expand the range and concept of his playing until he had become a virtuoso. "I didn't really start playing until I was nine. I guess I practiced, but I never considered it practice because I loved it too much. It was like searching in a new place you've never been before. I kept finding new things, new chords, new tunes." As this fascination and experimentation with the harmonica developed, Stevie had unwittingly taken the first step toward a career in music.

2. The Sound Of Detroit

Detroit is most commonly known as the center of the United States automobile industry, but its significance to America's black community may well be as important in the course of the nation's history. The city was a center of Abolitionist activity during the struggle against slavery in the early nineteenth century. For runaway slaves, Detroit was the last stop on the legendary Underground Railroad – across the Detroit river was Windsor, Canada, and freedom. In 1833, an outraged group of black citizens rescued Thornton Blackburn and his wife from a Kentucky sheriff who had come to Detroit to bring Blackburn back to slavery. The city had a respectable middle class black citizenry throughout its initial expansion, including the publisher of the Detroit *Plain Dealer*, Benjamin Pelham, known for his political influence as "The Czar of Wayne County".

By the early part of the twentieth century, however, the status of blacks in the city had deteriorated. As the auto industry grew by leaps and bounds, blacks were brought in to fill the dirtiest jobs for less money than other workers. During the 1920s Michigan gained the highest percentage of blacks of any state in the country; since housing was short, most of them lived in the most squalid conditions imaginable.

Many whites, particularly the recent European immigrants handicapped by a poor understanding of the language and competing for the same jobs, saw the incoming blacks as the enemy. By 1926 there were an estimated 875,000 Ku Klux Klan members in Michigan, the largest number in any state. The year before had seen an infamous racist incident which resulted in an important legal decision in the fight for black equality.

A black doctor named Ossian Sweet bought a house in a white neighborhood of East Detroit. The night after he moved in a hostile crowd of whites assembled outside the house and began throwing stones through the windows. Though a large group of police was on hand, they made no effort to disperse the angry mob, and as the situation grew uglier, the people inside the house panicked and fired several shots into the crowd, killing one man and wounding another. Dr Sweet and his companions were all arrested and charged with first-degree murder, but a brilliant defense by lawyer Clarence Darrow won an acquittal. Darrow later wrote, "The verdict meant simply that the doctrine that a man's house is his castle applied to the black man as well as the white man."

In the 1930s, the Great Depression ended the Detroit job boom and created even more intolerable conditions for the city's blacks. Dr. Sweet may have been acquitted, but the public had made its point. Detroit's own racial hate organization, the Black Legion, organized whites into an even more fearsome vigilante group than the KKK. Few blacks tried to move out of their strictly defined ghetto, and as their population increased their living conditions sickeningly declined.

In 1941, at the height of the struggle to organize auto workers into a union, Henry Ford's strong-arm terror coordinator Harry Bennett brought hundreds of destitute blacks into town from the South as strikebreakers. In exchange for promises of food, shelter and money, these men were persuaded to attack picket lines of white workers. The bloody exchange which ensued was typical of the way racial hatred and fear were cynically manipulated by employers and real estate speculators to keep the poor fighting among themselves instead of against the people who were making sure they remained in poverty.

When the United States entered the Second World War, Detroit had to gear up to supply the armed forces with an unprecedented number of tanks, trucks and planes. Another vast infusion of people hit the already critically overcrowded city when workers streamed in to fill the new jobs created by this increased demand for production. Housing was bad for all the workers, but it was worst for the blacks, and the real estate developers and vigilante groups did everything they could to keep it that way. Blacks were suddenly hired for positions that had previously been denied them in the work force, and for the first time found themselves eligible for the same promotions as white workers. Even though the United Auto Workers Union encouraged equal opportunity for all, white workers still objected to having blacks on their assembly lines, and this prejudice was fuelled by the racist organizations. It was not uncommon for workers to hear a Southern voice booming from a sound truck outside the factories: "I'd rather see Hitler and Hirohito win than work next to a nigger."

Disgusting rumours were circulated that Negroes communicated syphilis through any contact and that the disease could be contracted merely by touching the same machine that had been used by a black. White workers staged wildcat strikes wherever blacks were promoted to equal status, while for their part, blacks could hardly understand why they should fight in a war for European freedom when they were not free at home. One man told a reporter: "The army is going to take me to 'fight for democracy' but I would as leave fight for democracy right here. Here we are fighting for ourselves."

The powder keg had been lit. The problem was serious enough for the Federal Office of Facts and Figures (OFF) to send investigators to Detroit to determine if racial tensions there could hurt the war effort. Their report noted that the Detroit police "seem bent on suppressing the Negroes. It is exceedingly urgent that steps be taken in regard to this matter promptly. Indications are that the morale situation among the Negroes is becoming increasingly worse. And if race riots were to break out in Detroit, the feeling of the Negro that 'If I must die for democracy, why not here?' would tend to spread farther over the country."

The report was prophetic, but nothing was done about it at the time; a year later Detroit erupted into civil war. On 20 June, 1943, a riot broke out when tempers flared among 100,000 Sunday picknickers at Belle Island, a popular summer recreation spot located just outside of the city center on an island in the Detroit river, the same location where little Steveland Morris would a few years later have his first try with a real drum kit. Individual skirmishes between small groups of blacks and whites suddenly flared up when a large gang of whites, many of them sailors, began to beat up at random any blacks they could find.

A few miles away, in the heart of the black ghetto known as Paradise Valley, Louis Jordan and his band were in the middle of a hot set at the Forest Club when an unidentified man jumped on the stage and announced that whites were on the rampage at Belle Island. The reports were exaggerated — though no one had been killed at Belle Island, word on the street was that a mob of whites had thrown a black mother and child off the bridge, killing them both. Within minutes, the black ghetto was in flames, stores were looted, and white motorists coming through the area were stoned and, in several cases, killed.

By midnight, Detroit was in the grip of a full-scale race riot. Exaggerated reports of a gathering Negro army bent on the total destruction of whites in the city led to a nightmare scene in which mobs of whites thousands-strong roamed the city beating up blacks wherever they found them. Blacks were assaulted as they left movie

Left: *Berry Gordy Jr., founder of Motown Records.* Right: *Junior Walker (standing) and the All Stars, who toured with Stevie during the early Motown years. Their gutsy soul sound was unlike the usual Motown productions.*

theaters, pulled from their cars, and the cars were overturned and burned. Other blacks were chased and cornered, beaten senseless and left for dead on the streets. For the next few days gangs of whites systematically roamed the streets in search of black prey. Police seldom intervened. Streetcars were stopped at random by the angry mobs and blacks were pulled into the gutter and beaten.

When the dust finally settled, 34 people had been killed — 25 blacks and nine whites. Over two million dollars in property damage had been sustained, most of it in the black ghetto, which was left without stores and services, and many families were left homeless. The scars from this race war never really healed. Indeed the Detroit in which Steveland Morris grew up had still not recovered from the social aftermath of the 1943 riots; the hatred and miserable living conditions would prompt another uprising in the black community in 1967. But out of the ashes of disillusion and misery for Detroit blacks came a new pride and determination to make their own destiny — leaders like Malcolm X and the Rev. Dr. Martin Luther King crusaded to make blacks proud of their racial identity. While little Stevie was still too young to understand, forces were shaping that would prove to be primary influences on his later life.

Berry Gordy Jr. was fourteen years old at the time of the 1943 riots. His father had moved to Detroit from Georgia in 1922 and became a successful merchant, so the Gordys were not as badly off as many other Detroit blacks. Nonetheless Berry Gordy Jr. taught himself an important lesson from the riots. He decided that the only way to challenge racism and injustice was to work aggressively for personal goals, not just to accept a fate created by others. To his father's disapproval, Gordy Jr. applied this principle to his role in the family business. Gordy Sr. wanted his son to take part in his trade as a plastering contractor, but Gordy Jr. became a professional boxer instead.

Boxers from Detroit had a reputation for being hard-nosed because of the town's notoriously tough street action, but young Berry, who fought as a featherweight, used guile and agility

more than brute strength. He was a percussionist in the ring, using timing and a clever rhythmic pulse in his attacks that would surprise rather than overwhelm his opponents.

Gordy's boxing career ended when he was drafted to fight in the Korean War in 1951. Upon his release from the service two years later, Gordy opened a record store in Detroit, known as the 3D Record Mart. The store reflected his interest in jazz, but there was neither enough money nor enough interest among the local people to sustain the business, which eventually failed in 1955, and Gordy found work on the Ford assembly line. Married and with three kids, mortgaged to the teeth to keep his household going and subject to the harsh realities of a factory caste system that made it especially tough on blacks, Gordy found himself in exactly the position he swore he would never be caught in.

Gordy's wife, Thelma, sued him for divorce on the grounds of cruelty, claiming that she was repeatedly beaten up by Berry, and in 1957 the marriage broke up. Starting fresh, Gordy decided to try his hand at songwriting. He had been writing a bit in his spare time, and came into contact with a lot of local musicians at the Flame Show Bar, where his sisters held the cigarette concession. Two of Gordy's friends in the house band, Maurice King and Thomas Boyles, would eventually join Gordy's record company.

At first Berry Gordy found little success as a songwriter. His big break came when he discovered that an old friend from his boxing days, Jackie Wilson, had become a singer and was looking for material. Gordy wrote a handful of songs with help from his sister Gwendolyn and gave them to Wilson. One of the songs was *Reet Petite*, which became a substantial hit. Wilson wanted more, and Gordy came up with *Lonely Teardrops*, one of the biggest hits of 1959.

Berry decided to go into producing and publishing music, thus taking the first real steps toward establishing his own record company. With a used, beat-up recording machine and a smooth line of persuasion, Gordy set up a makeshift record company in his house. He would record anybody who walked in the door with a song and a hundred dollars. He and his second wife, Raynoma Liles, would often sing backing parts on the records.

Making records was one thing, but getting them played on the radio was more difficult. Gordy met an enterprising promotion man named Alan Abrams who wanted to work with him; Gordy was skeptical, so he gave Abrams a seemingly impossible task. One of his hundred dollar specials had been made with a Canadian singer from Yugoslavia. If Abrams could get *that* record played he could have the job. Abrams went and harassed a disc jockey so relentlessly that the jock finally played the record just to get him out of his hair. An astonished Gordy immediately hired Abrams, who was to become a key member of the Motown organization.

After *Lonely Teardrops*, Gordy became hot property. He followed it up quickly with a hit for singer Marv Johnson, *You've Got What It Takes*. But even with success, Gordy endured a lot of frustration as an independent record producer. No matter how good were the records he made, he would still have to hawk them round the major record companies, which involved a lot of his time and money. Then there was no guarantee that any company would agree with his appraisal of his own product, and beyond that,

Jackie Wilson gave Berry Gordy his first big break when Reet Petite *and* Lonely Teardrops, *both written by Gordy, became big hits in the late fifties.*

20

no certainty that they would correctly promote or distribute the records they did buy.

As Gordy realized that there was a wealth of black talent in Detroit with no place to go, he began to think about taking a chance and doing it all himself. One of the groups he had been working with was the magnificent vocal ensemble the Miracles, led by the awesomely talented Smokey Robinson. Gordy had already produced two Miracles singles written by Robinson, *Got A Job* and *Bad Girl*. Robinson was not just a gifted singer — he had a shrewd business sense, and saw that Gordy had the raw materials and the nerve to put together his own record company. Smokey urged Gordy on to this end, and with eight hundred dollars borrowed from his family, Gordy started his own record company, Tammie Records. As it turned out, that name had already been copyrighted, so he changed it slightly, to Tamla, and made Smokey Robinson vice-president.

On the face of it, Gordy was attempting the impossible. Without the money and political connections of record industry insiders, a new company — especially a black company — was bucking astronomical odds. But Berry Gordy had the tenacity to face those odds, and the co-operation of a talented group of people who decided to throw in their lot with him. The corporate name selected for this small scale recording industry was Motown, taken from Detroit's nickname, Motortown.

The Gordys were already familiar with the tradition of a family business, and they put all their energy behind Berry's new project. He formed a publishing company, Jobete Music, and put his brother Robert in charge of it. His sisters, Esther and Loucye, took care of Motown's administrative business. Even Berry Gordy Sr. helped out, working as the company's maintenance man.

Gordy's sister Gwendolyn was also in the music business. She had helped Berry write songs for Jackie Wilson, and later worked for Chess Records in Chicago. Chess distributed records released on the Anna label, named after yet another Gordy sister (the Miracles' *Bad Girl* was one of these records). At Chess Gwendolyn met Harvey Fuqua, who owned the labels Harvey and Tri-Phi. When Gwen and Harvey married, the Motown family expanded — the two later brought their companies in under Gordy's corporate umbrella. Motown took over distribution of Anna, Harvey and Tri-Phi, and Fuqua brought along some musicians he had known — Junior Walker and the All Stars, Marvin Gaye, the Spinners, Lamont Dozier and Johnny Bristol.

The fledgling organization set up shop in a hap-hazard collection of run-down houses on West Grand Boulevard. The old houses gave a homespun touch to the company and enforced the family image that Gordy wanted to project. Bedrooms were turned into offices; dining rooms became recording studios. On the front porch of one of the buildings Gordy proudly hung a big sign which read "Hitsville USA".

It was an apt nickname for Berry's brainchild. Gordy's uncanny instinct for hits manifested itself immediately with *Money*, which he wrote for Barrett Strong and turned into a Top 30 hit on the Anna label. Berry's motivation for this title was powerful: "At the time I was broke," he explained. Barrett Strong remembers the shoestring level on which the company was working when they made *Money*. "We were just a small company then. Most of the employees were musically inclined. We all got together, we were in the studio, we were playing around. I was playing the piano. The idea just sort of came around. We put our hearts into it and we worked on it day and night. We had a small band, we had a couple of guitars, we didn't have what we have now as far as instrumentation. So we used what we had the best way we knew how and cut *Money*."

In early 1961 Gordy was presented with the first of what would become a long string of gold records for the Miracles — *Shop Around*, on the Tamla label. Soon every black kid in Detroit knew of Gordy and he was constantly besieged by musicians who wanted him to listen to them. Many of the artists who came to the company were discovered in this fashion or by Motown-sponsored talent contests at schools and social clubs around the city. Gordy set aside one afternoon a week just to listen to the hopefuls that would trek to his office in search of their big break.

While Gordy was building Motown, in another district of Detroit Steveland Morris was becoming a local sensation. He would play with friends on front porches around his neighborhood, copying songs from the radio and fooling around with improvised material. "We did a lot

of social gatherings," he recalls, "and for the most part singing in alleys and singing on porches, and I hadn't really taken it serious because I was thinking of getting into other things. Like I wanted to be an electrician. I wanted to be a minister, or maybe a sinner.

"We used to get pretty big crowds of people playing on those porches. I remember this one time, ha, this lady who was a member of our church, she was Sanctified Holiness, but she was still a member of our church, the Whitestone Baptist Church, and she came along and she said 'Oh, Steve, I'm ashamed of you for playing that worldly music out here. I'm so ashamed of you.' Ha, I really blew it, boy. I'd been a junior deacon in the church and I used to sing solo at the services. But she went and she told them what I was doing and they told me to leave. And that's how I became a sinner."

On 25th and 26th Streets, Steve's remarkable voice and innovative harmonica playing cut through the air. Everyone in the neighborhood knew who he was. Stevie was particularly impressive when accompanied by a friend named John Glover. "John and myself formed a group called 'Stevie and John'. I would play bongos and John played guitar, and I'd sing and John would do some of the harmonies with me. We did a lot of songs from the fifties and sixties – *Once Upon A Time There Was Love, Why Do Fools Fall In Love, Bad Girl*. We did another Smokey song, *My Momma Told Me To Leave Those Girls Alone*. I remember the first Marvin Gaye song I heard was called *Mister Sandman*. I used to do *Mister Sandman*, imitating Marvin."

It was through John Glover and his mother Ruth that Stevie's reputation in the neighborhood blossomed. "I owe a lot to the neighbors we had. I owe a lot to the people we met, a lot to John Glover's mother, Ruth Glover, who actually was responsible for getting me to Motown and dealing with a lot of the things I was not aware of. Many times my mother was not aware of what I was doing because I would just go. I knew my way around the neighborhood pretty well. Just about every day John and I would meet and play and sing. So a lot of times my mother would have to go looking for me and try to find out where I was and what I was doing."

As luck would have it, one of Steve's friends was Gerald White, brother of Ronnie White, one of the Miracles. Gerald repeatedly asked his

Top: *The Supremes (left to right: Mary Wilson, Florence Ballard and Diana Ross)*. Left: *The Four Tops, who along with the Supremes, epitomized the Motown Sound*. Right: *Smokey Robinson (second from right) and the Miracles.*

brother to come over and listen to Steve and John Glover play, but Ronnie kept putting him off. Though White did not take his younger brother seriously at first, he finally agreed to stop by and see what all the fuss was about.

Ronnie White showed up with Pete Moore, another member of the Miracles. "We asked him to sing some tunes for us, right there in the living room," recalls Moore. "He said 'I can sing badder than Smokey', which cracked us up until he actually started singing *Lonely Boy*. He had such energy and feeling that we decided to set up a meeting for him with Brian Holland, who was a talent scout for Berry Gordy Jr at the time. There was barely a Motown Records then; Berry was just getting it together."

The next day White went to the office and told Holland about his find. Holland, one of the brilliant Holland-Dozier-Holland songwriting team, agreed to audition the kid, but when Stevie came to the studio there was a session in progress, so the audition took place on a Woodward Avenue stoop with only street noise for accompaniment. Most youngsters would probably have been rattled, but as soon as Steve put the harmonica to his lips he was in another world; he blew that sweet, ethereal sound culled from all the Jimmy Reed and Little Walter records he had memorized over the years. Holland was impressed. Steveland Morris had found a second home.

It was as obvious to Berry Gordy Jr. as it was to Holland and White that this extraordinary blind boy from the ghetto had enormous potential. But signing an underage child to a recording contract was not easy — Stevie needed a guardian's approval as well as supervision from the state labor authorities. If Steve had been less talented it might not have been worth the effort, but Gordy wanted to start shaping his career right away. The complex legal maneuverings were finally consummated when Steve signed a five-year contract giving Motown control over his recording, publishing and management, setting aside all his earnings until he became legally responsible at the age of 21.

3. Hitsville USA

The facilities at Motown were a dream come true for Stevie. There were more instruments laying around in the studio than he'd ever imagined existed. Every day after school he'd show up at the offices and stay until dark, practicing any instruments he could get his hands on — eventually becoming proficient on drums, organ and piano.

Stevie has a vivid recollection of his first exposure to the Hitsville studios. "People were just walking around relatively casually," he says. "There were some people working on songs in different rooms and I was taken into the main studio, Studio A, and I started playing the piano and singing. Somebody started playing drums and I said 'Oh, can I play those drums?' So I started playing drums."

Lula was a dutiful stage mother, shepherding Stevie around to and from the offices, watching over him as best she could. Though his money was to be held in trust until he turned 21, the provisions of the contract were still something of a windfall for Lula — Steve was provided a small allowance, what Motown nicknamed "carfare", and Lula was likewise allocated regular payments for his clothing and upkeep. To a poor, uneducated woman bred in a squalid ghetto, this alone was a blessing almost beyond comprehension. Certainly the work of God Himself, Lula decided.

Despite his mother's careful attention, Stevie managed to get off by himself during his forays to Motown and cause a little trouble. "It was like a music store with all kinds of toys — instruments for me to play. Me and my friend, after a couple of days we kept going down there, and we went in the basement and stole some tapes. This is something Motown probably never knew I did, but it's cool now. I stole — it must have been a two-track of *Shop Around* by the Miracles. I kept it — I think we tore it up or something. I don't know. But they were asking me 'Steve, have you seen it? Somebody stole a tape. Where's the tape?' And I just never did say anything about it.

'Cause I thought I'd lose my contract."

Stevie started recording sample tracks with a variety of producers almost immediately. Motown has been mythologized as a musical production line designed to imitate the efficiency of Detroit's automobile assembly lines, but this characterization isn't really accurate.

The automobile production lines were geared to produce the greatest number of cars in the smallest amount of time. Gordy's objective was to produce a limited number of high quality singles that could be counted on to be hits. He reasoned that a new company couldn't make it unless it demonstrated it could improve on the established commercial formula.

Gordy counted on inter-company competition to achieve his desired results. No writer or producer had sole jurisdiction over any one artist or group — they all had to compete until the best sound was arrived at. Gordy personally oversaw every aspect of this process and would not authorize a song for release until it had passed his stringent requirements.

This approach resulted not in a totally automated sound with interchangeable parts, but in a diverse musical identity that encouraged creativity. Of course, when Motown had success with one hit they would invariably follow it up with a succession of soundalike tunes until the idea had run its commercial course, but this is standard industry practice. For the most part, though, Motown records covered a wide variety of styles, especially the company's early days before the Holland/Dozier/Holland songwriting team struck a groove for the Four Tops and the Supremes. The records prove the point: the relentlessly driving pulse of *Money*; the smooth, melodic lilt of *Shop Around*; the bright, girl-group enthusiasm of *Please Mr. Postman*; the crude, insistent rock of the Contours' *Do You Love Me*; the explosive, barely controlled gospel emotions of *Stubborn Kind Of Fellow*, with its brilliantly fragile surprise element, a flute solo; the hypnotic sadness of *You Really Got A Hold*

On Me; the exquisitely arranged rhythm and blues of *Pride And Joy*; the smiling optimism of *My Guy*. One measure of the impact of this material is the fact that the Beatles recorded *Money, Please Mr. Postman* and *You Really Got A Hold On Me* on their second album, "With the Beatles".

The key to understanding the Motown sound is to realize that the company was closer to being a collective than a factory. The Gordy family philosophy extended to the employees as well. Despite the fact that they often signed over publishing and even performance money to the company in the standard contracts, few groups left Motown once they signed. The security of working with an all-black company was a considerable factor, as was Gordy's tireless presence and the sense that everyone at Motown was riding a winner.

Motown singles did have a certain common characteristic which led to the identification of a label sound. The makeshift studios where everything was recorded had an acoustic resonance which gave all the records a distinctively heavy, booming sound which was well suited to the driving rhythmic accent that was Motown's trademark. Although virtually everyone in the company had a hand in making its records —

Marvin Gaye often played drums on tracks when he wasn't singing, and Martha Reeves worked as a secretary before getting her chance to record for the label — Gordy employed the same crack players for as many sessions as they could cut. Most of the legendary Motown tracks were recorded with the rhythm section of drummer Benny Benjamin, bassist James Jamerson and keyboardist Earl Van Dyke.

The other constant in the Motown sound was Gordy's own involvement. No detail in the record making process escaped his attention. Despite the fact that Smokey Robinson was one of his most valued associates, Gordy is said to have rejected the first hundred songs Robinson wrote for Motown.

The late Marvin Gaye recalled that Gordy's assistance was crucial in turning *Stubborn Kind Of Fellow* into a hit: "I had written a jazz kind of thing on that, and Berry Gordy was in the control room at the time and he was listening to it. He said 'Well, now, let's change a few chords,' and we changed a few chords and he said 'Now it sounds pop, man. Now I think we can get some record sales out of it'."

Stevie presented Motown with unique recording problems. Because of his age and the special nature of his talent he had to have an almost

Some of Motown's money-spinners. Left: *The Temptations.* Above: *Marvin Gaye.* Right: *Smokey Robinson and the Miracles.*

complete sound tailored to him, unlike the company's older artists who could adapt themselves to whatever musical situation was required. Gordy worked through this process with a lot of patience, pairing Stevie with a variety of musical settings in an attempt to find a format that would highlight his genius appropriately.

It took more than a year before the sound began to take shape. Stevie had started writing songs even before joining Motown – he recalls that the first song he wrote was *Lonely Boy*, and that Motown originally let him record some of his own material.

"The first thing I ever recorded was called *Mother Thank You*, which originally was called *You Made A Vow*. They felt that *You Made A Vow* was too much a love song for me and they decided to change it." The song had a big band calypso sound, and Stevie's beautifully controlled singing was recorded perfectly to accent the sweet, almost girlish sound of his voice.

Mother Thank You was eventually retitled *Thank You (For Loving Me All The Way)*, and released much later as the B-side of *Castles In The Sand*, but most of the other material recorded during Steve's first year with Motown is lost to history. "When we first started out we did a lot of standard tunes which were never released because Motown wanted a single. At that time I worked with a gentleman named Clarence Paul as my musical director. He was basically a producer at Motown and the first one to really spend time working with me. Clarence was like a father, like a brother and a friend."

Gordy recalls Stevie's unusual talent and the special problems it posed. "I do remember seeing him," says Gordy of his first glimpse of the young musician. "Someone told me 'Watch this kid,' he was playing bongos and singing, doing very well. I didn't even know at that time that he could play harmonica as well as he could. I knew that he was very talented. I heard him sing and I felt that there was a uniqueness in his voice."

Though everyone at Motown was obviously impressed with Stevie's wide range of talents, it took the company a long time to figure out how to market him. The first album's worth of material he recorded was an instrumental concept called "The Jazz Soul of Little Stevie" intended to showcase his abilities as a multi-instrumentalist. The record was an investment in Stevie's future and a kind of practice session to work out which was the best direction to go with him. It's easy to see why Motown waited to release both this record and "A Tribute To Uncle Ray" until Stevie had a hit single.

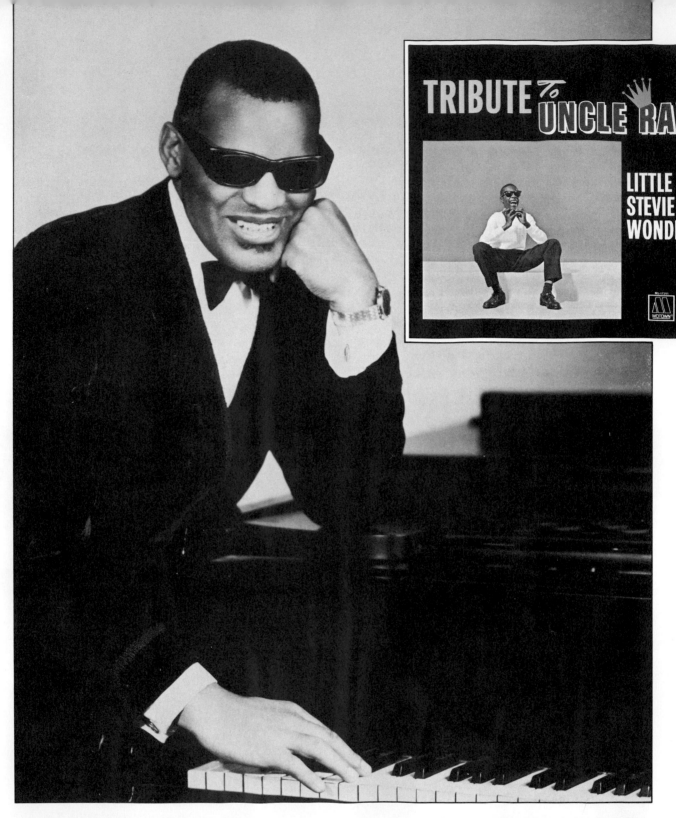

TRIBUTE To UNCLE RAY

LITTLE STEVIE WONDER

Producer Clarence Paul wrote most of the material on "The Jazz Soul of Little Stevie" with Henry Cosby, and wrote arrangements for a flashy big band to accompany Stevie. The results are unlike anything else Motown was doing at the time. The version of *Fingertips* which opens Stevie's first album bears little resemblance to the later edition that would become his first hit.

This was a big band Afro-Cuban sound built around an excellent flute solo, and Stevie's bongo playing is hardly the song's centerpiece. Stevie *is* featured on *Square*, playing harmonica against a Count Basie-style horn arrangement. He's clearly a harmonica virtuoso at this point with the characteristic sound he's become known for already fully developed. On *Soul*

Above: Ray Charles. Motown thought they could connect Stevie Wonder with the famous blind pianist by making Stevie's first album a tribute record (inset) "Tribute To Uncle Ray".

Bongo, written by Paul and Marvin Gaye, Stevie flashes good bongo playing in tandem with congas and trap drums. *Manhattan At Six* is a hot Latin track with Stevie on trap drums and another great flute solo.

Paulsby opens with a mellow harmonica solo, then contrasts sax and flute solos with more harmonica and some crude but rhythmically adept organ playing from Stevie. He moves through a pretty fair approximation of a Jimmy Smith solo, then ends up on organ. *Some Other Time* is a ballad built around a soulful harmonica solo. *Wondering* is a snappy little organ tune with more Jimmy Smith posturing, and was co-written by Stevie, as was *Session Number 112*, in which Stevie blocks out the theme on piano and takes a cool, bluesy harp solo. On Berry Gordy Jr's *Bam*, Stevie plays the uptempo blues theme on harmonica.

"The Jazz Soul of Little Stevie" was an indication of Motown's respect for this talented kid, but it was a hard way to introduce him to the public, especially when Motown was totally geared to producing hit singles. Without a hit, both "Jazz Soul" and his second album, "A Tribute To Uncle Ray" sat on the shelf until the summer of 1963 while the company tried to figure out how to break Stevie into the hit singles charts.

The campaign intended to link Stevie with Ray Charles through "A Tribute To Uncle Ray" was a failure. The company obviously hoped that the connection with an already successful blind and black singer would be the key to public acceptance. Stevie was game, and though his high, reedy voice at the time wasn't really suited to the sophisticated big band arrangements Paul was writing for him, he still managed to give a good account of himself.

In fact, "Tribute To Uncle Ray" showed that Stevie was a vocalist to be reckoned with. His bright, upbeat *Hallelujah I Love Her So* is downright precocious as he replaces Ray's name with his own in the song. There's a nice saxophone solo here, and again on *Ain't That Love*, which features excellent accompanying vocal harmonies, probably from the Marvelettes. The register of *Ain't That Love* is too low for Stevie's juvenile voice, but he hits the notes in a half strangled throat exercise. On the straight blues *Don't You Know*, he moves from the vertiginous squeal at the beginning to the gravelly throated lowdown delivery of the main verses. "Have you heard Stevie Wonder's in town?" he brags. "You can mess around till the midnight hour to see what's puttin' down." He goes on to throw in some strangely authentic sexual grunts and moans.

The Masquerade, a beautiful ballad extremely well suited to the character of Stevie's voice at the time, is the first example of the powerfully emotional ballad style that he would one day become famous for, whereas *Frankie And Johnny*, an adaptation of the folk song that has run through the American oral tradition, is a spirited gospel-style workout with a hot backing track. It has tremendous harmony vocal-group accompaniment and an octave-soaring performance from Stevie, who handles the narrative deftly.

He shows a maturity far beyond his years on his power-packed reading of the standard blues *Drown In My Own Tears*. It's hard to add something new to a song that has been sung so many times, but Stevie's is as good a version as you'll hear. Similarly, he caresses each note of Ray Charles' plaintive ballad *Come Back Baby* with all the feeling of a rejected lover, hitting bone-chilling high notes and bending his voice superbly for dramatic effect.

The big band arrangement of *Mary Ann* practically drowns Stevie harmonically, but shows that he could work fearlessly against a full brass section. *Sunset*, a moving ballad written by Stevie with Clarence Paul, is another *tour de force* for the boy, whose voice is backed by piercing harmony vocals and an extremely bluesy muted trombone phrase repeated over and over. The saxophone solo on the chorus is quite remarkable. Finally, Berry Gordy himself wrote *My Baby's Gone*, another medium-tempo crying blues with a melodic hook sung by the backing girl group in the Motown hit tradition. It's interesting that the company never released this song as a single.

In the end, Stevie's first single was finally released on 16 August, 1962. The name of the song was *I Call It Pretty Music (But The Old People Call It The Blues)*, written by Clarence Paul. It made little impact on the record listening and buying public, but it is interesting in that the label christened the boy "Little Stevie Wonder". "It was given to me by Berry Gordy," Stevie deadpans. "They didn't like 'Steve Morris', so they changed it."

4. The Twelve-Year-Old Genius

Stevie Wonder was the talk of Motown, but Steveland Morris was still just another student at Fitzgerald School for the Blind. School was at best a necessary evil, keeping Stevie away from his deepest interests, but he dutifully learned his Braille and showed a little interest in science and history. "It got kind of boring," he admits, "I guess because of the way it was put to us in books. The most interesting thing to me was about civilizations before ours, how advanced people really were, how high they had brought themselves only to bring themselves down because of the missing links, the weak foundations. So the whole thing crumbled. And that's kind of sad."

One of the biggest problems Stevie had at that point was that nobody really took his burgeoning musical career seriously. Motown could only be expected to carry him for so long without a hit single, and his parents and teachers were worried that Steve would build up unreasonable expectations only to be cruelly disappointed.

But Stevie never lost his confidence in himself, even when his second single, a duet with Clarence Paul called *Waterboy* was released on 3 October, 1962 and went nowhere. The song wasn't that good, but the flip-side, *La La La La La,* showed promise.

Then on 26 December, 1962, Motown released Stevie's first classic, *Contract On Love*, backed by a song called *Sunset*, which was co-written by Stevie and taken from the "Tribute To Uncle Ray" LP, which still hadn't been released. *Contract On Love* really showed what Stevie could do, starting out with percussive handclaps and a hot backing track with Stevie "strutting" his vocal, in total control. The Temptations provided fantastic backing vocals on the track. Though the song was only marginally more successful than his previous releases it showed that his sound was as commercial as anything else coming out of Motown.

Maybe the trouble was that Stevie couldn't express his full power in the studio format. His live performances, however, were astonishing. The stipulations of his contract prevented Stevie from playing clubs, so his opportunities to play live were limited to the packaged concerts that Motown would throw together from time to time. In these, Stevie consistently stole the show from such seasoned professionals as Marvin Gaye.

Stevie wasn't a particularly polished performer. He worked instinctively, building to an emotional frenzy on stage, and driving audiences crazy in the process. The Motown shows were slickly choreographed affairs, and Stevie's gospel-meeting outbursts swamped the proceedings. His great musical instincts translated to his backing group, and the session musicians responded to his improvisations with fierce playing. In a strictly timed show Stevie would run on well past his alloted segment, urging the band to play one more chorus as the audience shrieked in approval. On several occasions Clarence Paul had to go out on stage and physically carry the boy off to end his performance!

"The first time I began to feel I was exciting to people," recalls Stevie, "I threw my glasses out into the audience. I used to have a bow tie on, I threw that out, and that all stemmed from the time I did *Fingertips*. It was so exciting that I wanted to get them to do it again, so the next night I tried it again and it still was exciting."

The resourceful Gordy decided to record one of Stevie's live performances and see what would come of it. Again, this was against the grain of everything Motown had done up until this point, but it demonstrates how Gordy was prepared to experiment in the all-important business of producing hits.

Motown recorded Stevie's set at the Regal Theatre in Chicago, roughly an album's worth of material from "Jazz Soul" and "Tribute To Uncle Ray" (to be released as "The Twelve-Year-Old Genius"). The tracks from "Tribute" were unspectacular – though on *Don't You Know*, Stevie worked the audience skillfully, *Drown In My*

Own Tears, Hallelujah I Love Her So and (*I'm Afraid*) *The Masquerade Is Over* were better in the studio.

The rest of the material, though, was dynamite. *La La La La La* is much better than the studio version, a joyful, stomping romp with a good portion of the audience singing a call-and-response with Stevie on the happy chorus and a spirited percussion break led by Stevie on the trap drums. *Soul Bongo* is also an improvement on the original, with Stevie at his front porch best pounding away on the bongos, and the band responding behind him with a crisp, spirited rendition of the tune.

But the album's outstanding track by far is the revamped *Fingertips*, a performance that must stand as the high point of Stevie's early career. The song introduced Stevie's section of the Motown revue. "Right about now ladies and gentlemen," intones Motown MC Bill Murray, "we'd like to continue with our show by introducing to you a young man that is only twelve years old. And he is considered as being a genius of our time. Ladies and gentlemen, let's you and I make him feel happy with a nice ovation as we meet and greet Little *Stevie Won*-dah!"

The audience responds with sporadic cheers as congas and handclaps set up a groove and Stevie chants "Yeah . . . yeah," getting the feeling, then raps his intro over the music: "Ladies and gentlemen, now we're gonna do a song from my album 'The Jazz Soul Of Little Stevie'. The name of the song is called uh . . . *Fingertips*. Now I want you to clap your hands . . . c'mon . . . yeah . . . stomp your feet . . . jump up and down and do anything you *wanna* do . . . yeah *yeah* . . ."

Drums punch in, Stevie starts playing harmonica — short phrases of the intro — until the full band hammers in behind him and Stevie lays fluid, rhythmic lines through the bleating horns. Stevie's sustained solo travels through a couple of verses with shouting intensity, bleating percussive rasps on the instrument while the drums urge him on, until they blast through another chorus and Stevie starts shouting "Ev'rybody say *yeah*!" The whole theater rocks back with a deafening response of "Yeah." Stevie keeps it going: "Say Yeah!" ("Yeah". . .) "Say Yeah!" ("Yeah"), over and over until the climax, but instead of stopping, he goes right back into the harp solo, the band wailing behind him.

After another chorus he sings, "Just a little bit of soul-ol-ol-oh-oh-oh-ol yeah — yeahyeah — yeahyeah . . . clap your *hands* just a little bit louder . . . clap your hands just a little bit louder." Then back to the main theme, breaking to a harp solo with only handclaps for accompaniment over eight bars, then the full band comes in for another finale.

Except that once again Stevie won't stop, and starts singing again over rhythmic handclaps: "I know that everybody hey — yeah — everybody have a good t-ime . . . So if you *want me to* . . . if you want me to . . . I'm gonna swing this song — yeah — just a one more time . . ." Another blast of the theme builds to fever pitch with Stevie dragging his exit out for all it's worth: "Good*bye* goodbye good-*bye* goodbye good-*bye* good-*bye* good-*bye*." As a final sign-off Stevie switches from his blues solo into *Mary Had A Little Lamb* for comic effect, finally breaking the tension.

The confusion created by Steve's unwillingness to leave the stage added a tremendously dramatic touch to the sound. Because of the swift turnover of acts in the show, part of the next band ended up playing on the last section of *Fingertips*. The performance is the perfect amalgam of youthful optimism and raw power, and though the idea came from gospel, it's rock 'n' roll at its best.

"Mary Wells was next on the bill," says Stevie, "and it was time for her to go on, so what happened is that her bass player was getting situated and he came out and we were going

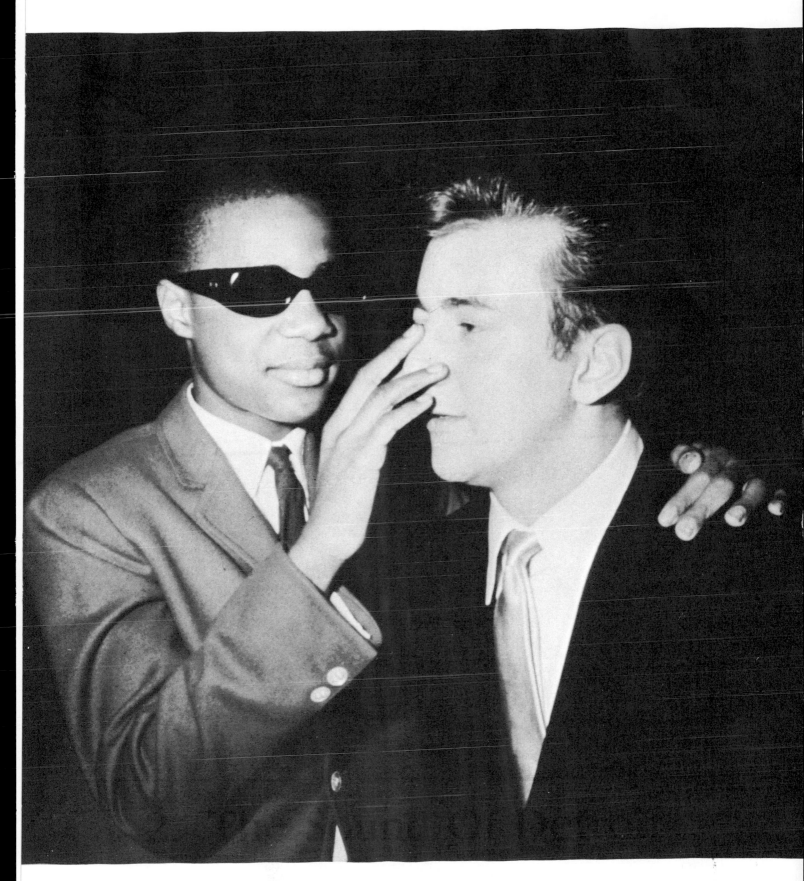

Stevie getting to know the late Bobby Darin in his own inimitable way.

says. "I can't remember it exactly, but the gist was: 'Anyone who can suggest a way for Stevie Wonder to go on the road and still continue his studies, please call Mrs. Morris.'

"A lady named Mrs. Helen Traub, who taught at a school for the blind, answered the ad. Through her we met Dr. Robert Thompson of the Michigan School for the Blind and he worked out a program for me, which included a private teacher, Ted Hull, who worked with me on the road. I spent two weeks out of the month at the Michigan School for the Blind, then when I was on the road I would do two hours a night, then I'd spend two weeks at home and I would work four hours a day. I always had homework to do. Fortunately it turned out really good."

Stevie's future as a musician was secure and he settled down into a carefree existence at Motown. "I was in a wonderful family situation at Motown and they took care of me. I was loved and encouraged.

"The first time I met Diana Ross — we called her Diane, then — I used to be in love with that chick, Jack. I don't know if I wanted to do it to

her, 'cause I was too young, but I sure was in love with that chick. I loved her to death. I used to have a fantastic crush on her. I loved her voice. I loved her talking voice. I used to listen to the tune *Time Changes Things* over and over again for thousands of hours *wishing* that I would meet a girl like that. I did!

"Martha Reeves and I used to sit up all the time and make up tapes and songs and stuff. And I borrowed about three Motown tape recorders that never came back. Every year we used to have Christmas parties, Motown Christmas parties, and they were really always outasite. Everybody from the company would come and we'd have 'em in the studio, the recording studio itself, and we'd tear up the studio. Partyin' back."

The playfulness Stevie exhibited in his childhood days at home developed into more elaborate games at Motown. He would constantly make jokes about his blindness and pretend to trip and fall. He was also an inveterate practical joker. "Thank goodness they all loved me as much as they did. I loved to play jokes on everyone. I knew the intercom numbers of everyone at Motown and I'd change my voice and say things like 'This is Berry and I want you to get Stevie that tape recorder right away. He's a great new artist so it's okay to spend the money and buy it for him. I'm sure he'll get it back to us in a few days.' After they fell for this stunt about three times and never got the tape recorder back, they gave me a recorder as a belated birthday present."

On 13 September, 1963, Motown released Stevie's next single, *Workout Stevie Workout*, backed by *Monkey Talk. Baby Workout* had been one of Jackie Wilson's hottest numbers, and while *Workout Stevie Workout*, written by Clarence Paul and Henry Cosby, was not particularly imitative of the Wilson tune, it definitely had a similar feel. It was the most unabashedly gospel piece of material Stevie recorded for Motown, with a tremendous gospel backing group playing against his own impassioned vocal and some nimble harmonica playing over an extremely spirited backing track. The record hit the Top 30 which wasn't bad, especially since *Fingertips Part II* was still getting a lot of airplay, but the most important thing about *Workout Stevie Workout* was that it proved Stevie Wonder could capture the magic of his live performances in the studio.

Above: *Martha Reeves and the Vandellas. Martha was a particular friend to Stevie who had his own share of pressures during this time, as he was obliged by law to continue his education while on tour.*

5. Stevie At The Beach

The era of "Little" Stevie Wonder ended almost as soon as it began. When Clarence Paul brought the boy into the studio in late 1963 to record his fourth album, "With A Song In My Heart", he soon discovered that Stevie's voice was beginning to break, dropping in register as he grew. After deciding what material to include on the record, Paul recorded all the backing tracks keyed to Stevie's vocal pitch. Because of the touring schedule Stevie had to wait until after his next tour to sing the final vocals for the album, but when he got back into the studio his voice had already lowered so much he was unable to sing in the register in which the songs had originally been recorded.

The results were less than spectacular, but in a way it didn't matter. Even if Stevie had been in top form for this session, the material was just inappropriate for him. Every number was a supper club standard, recorded with schmaltzy MOR strings and soulless backing vocals — Stevie at the dentist's office. Why Motown could make an album like this after taking so much trouble to establish his reputation as a hot rocking live performer defies explanation.

Certainly the songs in question are classic crooning material — the title track, *When You Wish Upon A Star*, *Smile*, *Make Someone Happy*, *Dream*, *Put On A Happy Face*, *On The Sunny Side Of The Street*, *Get Happy*, *Give Your Heart A Chance*, and *Without A Song* — and Stevie delivers it all with great feeling, but the stultifying arrangements really detract from his performance. In the long run, though, it was probably good for Steve to work as hard as he did on material like this. Even in failure, the melodic and harmonic training he got singing on this album certainly helped to shape his own ballad style. You can hear intimations of Stevie's later greatness on his interpretations of *On The Sunny Side Of The Street* and *Smile*.

In live performances Stevie's voice change was masked by having him sing duets with Clarence Paul on all the ballads. The uptempo numbers posed no problems because Steve didn't have to hit pure high notes and hold them, and he could bend his voice on fast tunes like a pro. With the help of Martha Reeves he improved his stage presence by learning all the latest dance steps from her. "We used to do finales that were out of sight," says Stevie. "Martha Reeves used to show me all the new dances to do. She would say 'Yeah, this is ba-ad, this will make you look sexy on stage.' I tried to do splits and I did The Hitchhike and all the latest stuff. Martha would always show me the baddest steps." Stevie appeared on the two live anthologies released in 1964, "Motor Town Revue Vols 1 & 2", singing *Don't You Know* on the former, then a rocking *I Call It Pretty Music (But The Old People Call It The Blues)* and *Moon River* on the second volume.

Life on the road was a gas for the boy. "Suddenly I was surrounded by older people all the time, and there were temptations. Like, I wanted to stay up late at night but I had a chaperon who made sure I went to bed."

Ted Hull, the official liaison from the Michigan School for the Blind, worked so closely with Stevie that he was virtually acting as his personal manager. Hull started working with Steve in September, 1963, and stayed with him through his formative musical years. "Motown recruited me," Hull explains. "They did a nationwide search looking for a suitable tutor for Stevie. I was totally in charge of Stevie's day to day activities. The company, working through a booking agent, would consult with me and set up a tour. Then it was my job to provide Stevie's educational needs as coordinated through the School for the Blind.

"It was also my job to manage Stevie's day-to-day business affairs, and so we would travel throughout the country or around the world with a lot of activities. I was paid by Motown, and the management part of Stevie's program was directed by Motown. All I had to go on was my own childhood, and so I established an allowance with Stevie and I worked it out with his parents so he didn't develop champagne tastes at too early an age. It seemed to work very well. He seems to appreciate it now, but he didn't appreciate it at all at the time.

"One of my positions with Stevie was — he was traveling a lot with us, so his food, his clothing, his day-to-day needs were taken care of. There was always money filtering through from other sources, and so we really had to tighten up a little more than I would have maybe on my own son. Because, you know he had a little leverage himself, a little political clout with his parents or with the company, but it turned out very healthy — it worked out very well."

Traveling conditions posed no problems for Stevie. He adapted well to the nightly switch of hotel rooms. "Shortly after traveling," he says, "you find that most hotels are made the same and you can only get so much in a room — a bedroom, a closet, a bed and a bathroom, maybe another closet or whatever. You know where everything is going to be, you know where the telephone is going to be."

During the early Motown tours Stevie developed the habit of working on almost no sleep, spending late night hours writing songs and developing new musical ideas. "All the groups would be on the bus, and the thing I remember about Stevie," recalls a member of the Contours, "is that when everybody would be sleeping Stevie would be back in the back of the bus, and he would always want you to hear something, and it would always be so good and so you had to kind of wake up and listen to him. He was just budding, but he had so much talent it was only a question of which direction he wanted to go."

Stevie took a child's delight in what older musicians would have certainly considered a gruelling schedule. For Stevie it was enough just to be surrounded by so many musical legends. "Junior Walker was on the bus," he recalls with still a trace of unbridled happiness. "The parts of the tour that the Supremes did they were on the bus, the Vandellas, Marvin, the Tempts. We had lots of fun. I remember they used to call me Little Nappy Wonder."

"I was on a lot of the Motown tours with Stevie," says Junior Walker. "We used to joke around all the time. At the time he was on the tour he was going to school, you know, he had a tutor, a guy with him all the time who was teaching him. I would always joke with Stevie when I'd be going out at night. I'd come by his room and knock on the door, and he'd open the door, and I'd say 'Hey Steve, you wanna go out wit' me?' And he'd say, 'Yeah, man, where you goin'?' and I'd say, 'Well, I don't wanna tell you, you kids have to stay in.' I said, 'I seen a little chick out there that dug you.' He said 'You get her and bring her back to the room.' I said, 'Yeah, OK, Stevie.'"

The other members of the Motown entourage were charmed by Stevie and amazed at how well he got around. "You would never look at him as being handicapped," says Smokey Robinson. "I recall when we used to take Motortown revues to places like the Apollo and theaters like that and his dressing room would be on the fourth floor. By the second or third day he was running around backstage at the Apollo just like everybody else, like he could see."

"He would come in," adds Junior Walker, "he'd know my voice. I could be sittin' there talkin' to someone and he'd say — 'There's that old Jr. Walker boy! That old 'Shotgun' boy! Stevie could *hear* you ... anybody in here that he had talked to once before, you couldn't trick him. He'd know me wherever I was, wherever I'd be. Even in a crowd of people, he'd know you. He'd say 'I know the Roadrunner's in here somewhere. Jun-ior?' And then he'd push his way through the crowd and come to me."

Stevie played his part as mascot and prankster to the hilt. "I was maybe a little brother to a certain degree," he admits. "Some of that may be over-emphasized but there were things I did do that were mischievous, that young children do."

No one was immune from Stevie's practical jokes, not even the women that he adored. "He was like my little boy," says Dionne Warwick, before setting up the story of one of Steve's most outrageous pranks. "I'll never forget what he did to me one evening. He was standing in the backstage area. I had a dress that the Shirelles hated. The Shirelles told Stevie, obviously without my knowledge, 'Stevie, we want you to do something for us.' And they put him up to this little ruse. Stevie had a way of identifying me from my scent — I'd wear Shalimar and he'd always know it was me — 'Here comes Dionne,' he'd say. So I said 'Hello baby, how are you today?' He says 'Dionne, I don't like that red dress.' Well it scared me, because I know he's

The Four Tops (Lawrence Payton, Duke Fakir, Obie Benson and Levi Stubbs) had their first Motown hit in 1964.

Tops and the Temptations and Martha and the Vandellas and the Supremes and so forth and we would have to go in the back entrance of restaurants and eat in the kitchen — that wasn't very long ago — and go to hotels that had booked us and you know when they find they've got black people coming in suddenly they can't find your reservations. I was generally the only white man on the bus, so I had to do what I could to make it work but I didn't have a lot of experience. I wasn't really taking it all that seriously either because everybody had such a good sense of humor. See, if you didn't laugh at it, you couldn't endure it."

Stevie is philosophic about the racial problems he encountered in those days: "Down in Alabama, somebody shot a gun at the bus and just missed the gas tank. So you can understand why there's a feeling, I guess in some artists, there's a feeling of bitterness, because it was such a close-knit thing and then as the world changed and the company changed it was difficult to keep up that kind of family relationship.

"I remember once in Macon, Georgia, in 1963 or 1964, before things got any kind of together down there, there was a Confederate flag hanging over the stage. We had this cat, Gene Shelby, and he told this one guy, 'Our big star Marvin Gaye ain't gonna like that flag.' This guy says 'Hey, boy, see the way that flag's blowin' in the breeze? If you don't get your tail out of here, your tail's gonna be up in a tree blowin' just like that flag.'"

When Stevie wasn't on the road, Ted Hull still had to ensure that he stuck to a rigid schedule of tutoring: "We set up a rule of thumb, whereby if we were in the state and available for, let's say, 30 days, I would do the best I could to get Stevie in school for two weeks out of a four week period. We travelled an awful lot, so we didn't probably average two out of every four weeks. But I'm sure he averaged 50 per cent of the time we were in Michigan at the School for the Blind."

Stevie's unusual schedule kept him out of phase with the other students at the school. "He was in school probably at most three or four weeks at a time," says his Braille teacher, Lucille Kerner. "He'd be gone for three to four months."

George Anderson, who taught Industrial Arts at the School for the Blind, recalls that Stevie was never in his class long enough to make anything. "He was in my class but he really wasn't

blind and there's no way in the world this kid can see this dress, but if he didn't like it, I'm takin' it off. I never wore that dress again. It took two or three years before the Shirelles finally broke down and told me what they had done. So I'll never forget Stevie for making me throw away my $3.98 dress."

Traveling with the Motown revue also gave Stevie a whirlwind education in American race relations during the sixties. Ted Hull recalls that aspect of Stevie's education vividly. "My experience with Stevie was from '63 to '69 and that was right during the height of all the racial problems that we were having in this country. It's never been that exciting since. I remember the Four Tops taking pot shots at some guy trying to steal a suitcase off our bus. We definitely did have racial problems that were very maturing to me. One time I took Stevie to Memphis to do some shows and, holy smoke, that was really humiliating. We went on several Motown one-nighters on the bus with the Four

Above: Dionne Warwick, a long-time friend of Stevie's in spite of being the victim of his practical jokes.

42

there very often. He was always on the road. He'd be there maybe one day and then he'd be gone somewhere else."

Stevie's presence in other school activities was more pronounced. Choir director Yvonne Wainwright remembers him well. "He sang in the choir. He came in and sang tenor in the choir when he was in town. We had 45 singers in the choir at the time. We had Christmas programs, we did the traditional things. He was featured one Christmas singing *White Christmas*."

Choir was one subject Stevie's protracted absences didn't hurt. "With his ability he would quickly learn whatever he missed," explains Wainwright. "There was no problem."

One thing his teachers all agree on is that Stevie got along well with the other students. "He was a very appreciative boy," says Kerner. "Very polite, very religious." "He was a nice guy," adds Anderson.

"I remember some nice things," Yvonne Wainwright recalls. "There would always be the student who would want him to hear what they could do, perform, or what they had created, and he would always take the time to go down to one of the practice rooms and listen to them, which I thought was very generous and kind. He never refused to be kind to the other students and to listen to their ability. That was the one thing that stuck out in my mind, that he was very kind and generous with his time."

According to Hull, the social aspects of the program were the most important things the School for the Blind offered Stevie. "You're trying to do the best for the child at the time, and we felt that that was best because only at the School for the Blind could he have some normal life. The education was good, but the thing it gave him was the opportunity to make lasting friendships, and he did. God help us without friends. Friends to me are almost more important than family ties."

As far as Stevie was concerned the social life at the School for the Blind was an unqualified success. "When I did go back to school," he says, "they had everything, like swimming, boating, skating. I was on the wrestlin' team for a while, on the track team for a while, we got into various outside activities. I was more interested in music. But it was a challenge."

While Stevie wasn't actually at school, Ted

Hull really had his hands full. "I was exhausted most of the time," Hull admits. "He held out extremely well and I always recognized that Stevie was holding down two full-time jobs, one as a student and the other as an entertainer. I don't think he realized it. We wouldn't start school until about ten o'clock in the morning, but I would get up at 6 am usually to prepare for school – try to get a head start on the kid. Then we would have school for three and a half to four hours and then it would be the entertainment business until maybe twelve or one o'clock that evening. So I was absolutely exhausted, and in those early days we didn't have a valet and we didn't have a driver and it was tough. I would have to, on many occasions, hire the band and arrange for rehearsals and pay them off. It was tough."

The list of responsibilities that fell on Hull at the time was formidable. "I was the road manager," he explains. "I had all of Stevie's road management responsibilities and also a lot of his

Above: Although Stevie's star was in the ascendant, by the end of 1964 his voice was on the way down.

personal management responsibilities, because I was probably closer to the family and closer to Stevie than anybody else, and of course I had to coordinate the educational activities and the business activities. So I had to work for the Board of Education and the School for the Blind and Motown, and I made a lot of people mad.

"We had a good time, we really did. He taught me a lot also, and of course I learned a lot, being a minority, always being introduced as 'Ted — oh, that's the white guy over there.' Motown was never, ever critical about my expense accounts or anything and they were extremely pleased that they had a man who could just handle the job. They never called me on the carpet and cussed me out or that kind of thing even though I made it tough for them. I really did make it tough for them. A lot of times I wouldn't agree to let Stevie go on a job or I wouldn't agree to let Stevie stay at the recording studio past eight o'clock at night.

"I think maybe the nicest compliment I could pay Stevie as a student is that he was normal, a normal student. He responded to pressure in a normal way. He responded to criticism, he responded to praise. He was a very normal person, and if I can't say anything better than that about anybody I guess I'll stop right there. I hoped the program that Dr. Thompson and myself and Mrs. Edwards put together for Stevie would cause this kind of thing to happen. I'll tell you, there are some crazy people out there. When you've got hundreds of thousands of people a year telling you how great you are, I would probably think I was pretty good."

The last title released by Motown under the name "Little" Stevie Wonder was *Castles In The Sand*, a very unseasonal beach music single when it came out on 15 January, 1964. *Castles In The Sand* is a medium tempo ballad, opening with seaside surf sound effects and a Phil Spectorish production, featuring a crisp backing track and string arrangement, great rhythm guitar accents and a smooth Stevie in his crooner's role delivering a slick and assured performance. Commercially it was a flop, but it did usher in a brief and bizarre era of Steve's career. The beach music craze was hitting its peak and surf groups like the Beach Boys and Jan and Dean were popular, so Gordy decided to try Stevie out in this genre long enough to make a couple of B-movies and a beach music theme LP, "Stevie At The Beach". Stevie appeared in two of American International Pictures' beach movies, *Muscle Beach Party* and *Bikini Beach*. Both were standard follow-ups to *Beach Party*, starring Annette Funicello in her most famous role as Dee-Dee, the curvy beach bunny in love with Frankie Avalon. The cheesy naivety of these films has made them kitsch classics, but Stevie Wonder's appearance at the end of each picture is the musical high point of the proceedings, especially the *Fingertips* segment of *Bikini Beach*.

"Stevie At The Beach" was an improvement on "With A Song In My Heart" but still fell far short of being the proper vehicle for his talents. Two versions of *Castles In The Sand* were included, the single and an instrumental version — the identical backing-track with Stevie playing the theme on harmonica instead of singing it. A dramatic production of *Ebb Tide* is another of the four instrumentals on the album, based around an excellent harmonica solo, as is the hot track, *The Beachcomber*, and an awkward version of *Red Sails In The Sunset*.

Sad Boy is a good ballad with many self-references, showing off Stevie's more mature voice with great potential especially set against this lush, Spectorish production by Dorsey Burnett. *Happy Street*, an uptempo gospel tune, turns on fantastic drumming, a burning harmonica solo, handclaps and shouted "Hallelujahs" from the excellent vocal harmony group. *The Party At The Beachhouse* plays off the beach music sound with a heavy funk guitar pattern. The call-and-response chorus contrasts with an energetic, impromptu, almost scat vocal from Stevie with horns punctuating a flourish every eight bars. The track, with its overlays of swinging horn charts, boogie ryhthm pattern, breakneck harmonica solo and wild shouting, approximates the intensity of Stevie's live performances.

Beachstomp, part of the popular "dance song" genre of the early sixties, is based around a typical soul music brass arrangement of the time: single held trombone notes droning with trumpet blasts laid on top of them. It's a nice, tuneful arrangement but somehow Stevie is unconvincing as he sings about the joys of surfing. This is the kind of formula writing of which Motown was always being accused, but it's interesting to note that this record is totally unlike the Detroit based productions of Stevie's

early hits.

For some reason it was decided to include *Somewhere Beyond The Sea*, which stretched the beach music concept a bit thin. This standard, which is usually associated with various Italian-American crooners, strained Stevie's voice to breaking point at its highest registers. It simply should not have been included.

Hey Harmonica Man was designed as a single to showcase Stevie's identity. The vocal is dominated by a gospel-style chorus which, with its pronounced bass vocal punctuations and church meeting swing, was unlike other Motown pro-

ductions of the time in its calculated raggedness. Stevie jives and solos on the harmonica, but doesn't sound all that comfortable.

Though Stevie enjoyed visiting California, the calculated emptiness of the film projects and "Stevie At The Beach" seemed to disturb him. He obviously felt that whatever his musical future was, it wasn't shucking and jiving with archaic minstrel show accompaniment for an audience defined by Annette Funicello and Frankie Avalon. He later admitted that *Hey Harmonica Man* was an embarrassment to him, and referred to it as to a low point in his recording career.

Even at age thirteen, Stevie's instrumental skills were phenomenal; he could pick up techniques and harmonies by ear whether on piano, harmonica, bass or drums.

6. Uptight

In the first half of the 1960s, while a technological, artistic and political new wave swept across the globe, the United States made historic advances in the legislation of human rights. On 19 October, 1960, the Reverend Dr. Martin Luther King was arrested following a demonstration at several racially segregated lunch counters in Atlanta, Georgia. Dr. King had emerged as a leader of the civil rights movement five years earlier when he organized a successful boycott of the Montgomery, Alabama, bus system after a black woman was arrested for refusing to give up her seat on the bus to a white person.

Martin Luther King was a powerful religious figure as well as a political force because he championed a non-violent protest that added weight to his demands for justice. Dr. King's emotional, visionary speeches stirred a country made optimistic by the youthful idealism of President John F. Kennedy. Meanwhile Congress enacted legislation to enforce the Voting Rights Act of 1957, which was designed to give the franchise to southern blacks who'd been denied the right to vote. Kennedy proved a staunch defender of human rights when he backed up the decision to allow James Meredith, a young black student, to enroll in the previously segregated University of Mississippi.

Racial violence, almost always incited by whites and in some cases by the police, accompanied civil rights demonstrations, making Dr. King's non-violent stance all the more important. His 1963 "I Have A Dream" speech became a psychological turning point in public opinion about segregation. Even though President Kennedy was assassinated in November, 1963 his and Dr. King's dream lived on – in 1964 a bill outlawing racial discrimination of any form was passed into law. Dr. King was awarded the Nobel Peace Prize in 1964.

The spirit of idealism, that justice would prevail, provided the heady, optimistic social climate that prevailed when Motown (and the Beatles) defined the sound of an era. Stevie was a big part of this new spirit on the Motown road shows, where the painful realities of this social climate often intruded, but was increasingly estranged from the Motown magic on record.

Though Motown had officially dropped the "Little" from Stevie's name, the company still could not capture his commercial potential in hit singles. *Fingertips Part II* had been a number one hit, but it was a one-shot live recording and none of Stevie's studio singles even approached its impact, while the concept LPs Motown built around Stevie had all been failures except the live album.

Nevertheless, Wonder's live performances continued to be the most dynamic moments of the Motown revue. In March of 1964 the first Motown revue tour of England and Europe took place. Stevie, Martha and the Vandellas, Smokey Robinson and the Miracles and special guests Georgie Fame and the Blue Flames made up the show, and Stevie impressed the audience as well as the critics, with one enthusiastic English reporter commenting Stevie "bounds on stage in a gold Mohair suit and plays a possessed version of *Fingertips*."

Stevie had appeared on both the *Ready Steady Go* and *Thank Your Lucky Stars* television shows in England a couple of months earlier, but all the exposure did little to promote his record sales. A second tour with the Motown revue early in 1965 yielded similar results – good concerts but no record sales.

Part of this problem was undoubtedly that Steve's voice was changing, but the protracted lack of hit success was causing rumblings at Motown. One vice-president openly lobbied for Stevie's dismissal from the label. Stevie is philosophic about it now, but it must have been terrifying at the time. "No more Little Stevie Wonder," he laughed recently at his recollections. "I knew I wasn't as productive as I had been. I listened to WNRL and said 'Mommy, they not playin' my record no more.' Motown noticed that too. One guy at Motown, who eventually got fired, recommended that several Motown acts be dropped. 'One in particular we should drop is Stevie Wonder,' he said. 'His voice is changing, he's getting taller, we gotta buy him new clothes ... where's Michael Jackson when we need him?' So he would call me in and ask me to sing with strings, he'd say 'Sing over this' and I'd say, 'Make it a little lower, man, my voice is changing'."

Steve's ability to laugh at himself in retrospect is great, but if it wasn't for Berry Gordy this critic (whoever he was) might have gotten his way. Gordy had anticipated trouble with Stevie when he signed him, but figured the risk was worth it. "I remember that he was at such a young age," says Gordy, "that his voice had to change and that we were scared that his voice was gonna change, like all voices do, for the worse. It did change, he got a deeper voice and so forth but it changed for the better so we were very excited by that."

Gordy bought time while waiting for the transformation by releasing another live single. After *Hey Harmonica Man* and *Happy Street* stiffed in 1964, Gordy recorded the Motown revue again in 1965 at a Paris show. The record would be released in late 1965 as "Motown Revue In Paris", but Gordy clipped Stevie's version of *High Heel Sneakers* from it as a single and released it in the US on 2 August, 1965.

The *High Heel Sneakers* single offers an interesting contrast to *Fingertips*. At the cue, a

French announcer struggles with a bilingual introduction that boils down to "The big ... Stevie Wonder". Stevie starts his rap as tambourines and handclaps set up a testifying groove for him. Where on *Fingertips* he was the ebullient child prodigy, here Stevie is the cool seasoned professional. His voice sounds calculated as he sings "Now I want *everybody* to clap your hands ... *C'mon* – ah yeah – ahhhh *yeah*. Now let me get myself together ..." He carefully plays a simple blues figure on the harmonica until the band jumps in with a sweating bass and drum pattern and a grooving organ accompaniment. Stevie sings the chorus in his deepest natural register, mellowing like a horn as he shouts and twists the lyrics skillfully, playing off the driving rhythm. As the horns phase out an answering pattern of riffs on the chorus, Stevie swings a deft harmonica solo over them before returning to the verse for a rousing finale.

The tune is dynamic and slick at the same time, not a total outpouring of emotion like *Fingertips*, but a carefully controlled performance emblematic of the classic style that Stevie had developed during the course of 1965. Yet the control in *High Heel Sneakers* came completely from Stevie himself. "It was *live*," he says, "and it's all such a different thing live. *High Heel Sneakers* was, like, the highlight of the show. A lot of that had to do, too, with the musicians we were using then. They were French musicians playing with us and the guys couldn't understand English, they were just following along. It was a very spontaneous thing."

Stevie was an avid listener, and like a lot of other people in the sixties was strongly affected by the Beatles. As the Beatles stormed through America in 1965, Stevie realized that Motown's search for his style mostly went in the wrong directon. While his voice changed, so did his ideas about what he should be playing.

"I never felt that I strictly embodied the Motown sound," he says. "I had the independence because I was somewhat distant, because I was in school, and I would just come back home sometimes and do some singing. Clarence Paul, who was my arranger and conductor when I had the big group – we would work out doing tunes, ridin' in cars in England around '65. We'd think of different songs like *Funny How Time Slips Away* or *Blowin' In The Wind*."

Stevie realized that the key to avoid being

Stevie's new-found sophistication in the mid-sixties led him to experiment with his own songwriting.

pigeonholed at Motown was the material you recorded. "The sound wasn't really Motown as much as the writer," he explains. "I think for the most part they [writers] should listen in advance and know the artists. Holland/Dozier/Holland would sing the melodies themselves and say 'This is how I want you to do it.' Writers are so important."

The songwriting team of Brian Holland, Lamont Dozier and Eddie Holland came up with all of the hits by the Supremes and Four Tops in the mid-sixties — *Back In My Arms Again, Nothing But Heartaches, I Hear A Symphony, My World Is Empty Without You, You Can't Hurry Love, Where Did Our Love Go, Baby Love, You Keep Me Hanging On*, for the Supremes; *I Can't Help Myself, Reach Out I'll Be There, Standing In The Shadows Of Love, Bernadette*, for the Four Tops. Holland/Dozier/Holland had a lot to do with establishing Motown's identity, but Stevie was critical of the fact that they wouldn't involve the artists who were going to record their material in the writing process.

"I think a lot of our artists could have been more sustained if they had other writers," says Stevie, "besides Holland/Dozier/Holland, because then they would have found their identity — and that's what everybody needs."

Stevie knew instinctively that the best way to arrive at that identity was to write the songs yourself. Fortunately there were people at Motown who believed in his ability to do this, so Stevie was given a chance to dictate his own musical direction up to a point. Along with producer Henry Cosby and lyricist Sylvia Moy, Stevie worked hard to write hit singles. The three would have brainstorming sessions at every opportunity. Stevie already had a reputation for coming up with spontaneous licks and riffs on the bus during Motown tours (the flip side to *High Heel Sneakers, Music Talk*, had been written with tutor Ted Hull in one of those sessions). Cosby and Moy tried to come up with concepts that would fit Stevie's basic ideas.

It didn't take them long to arrive at an almost perfect result. Two months after *High Heel Sneakers* Motown released the song that is probably most identified with Stevie Wonder, *Uptight (Everything's Alright)*. The idea for the tune had germinated during one of the songwriting sessions; Stevie came up with the jubilant, hand-clapping chorus and the others quickly constructed a song around it.

It is significant that Henry Cosby took over the production responsibilities from Clarence Paul on this track. Paul was the consummate professional in Motown's production group, a sophisticated musical mind adept at big band arrangements and Vegas-style slickness. Cosby, however, was a more instinctive producer, who felt the deep-rooted rhythm patterns of the Motown session band. He was skilled at catching the sound compression that was such a big part of the intensity associated with the Motown sound.

In 1965, the Motown rhythm section — drummer Benny Benjamin, bassist James Jamerson and keyboardist Earl Van Dyke — really came into its own, carving out the big beat Motown trademark on records by the Supremes and the Four Tops. *Uptight* was clearly in this same groove.

The first thing you hear when you play the record is the snare drum pulse that propelled Motown to its legendary status as incomparable dance music, then the rolling bass pattern pushing it along, fuzz guitar picking out distinctive accents against the rhythm until the clarion trumpets state the melodic theme that heralds Stevie's triumphant vocal entrance into the song.

Uptight established Stevie Wonder's identity. The absence of harmonica or other gimmicks to promote him is pointed — Stevie is presented in the tune on his own, shouting his joyful, life affirming message. Stevie portrays himself as an outcast from ideal society. "In every pocket you can see I'm a *poor man's son*." But while he points out all the things he isn't, Stevie argues that his life is richer because his heart is true. Stevie is jumping out of his skin with joy, simply because he is alive and feeling the warmth and love of inner happiness.

Stevie looks back on *Uptight* as the major turning point in his evolution into the Motown system, and singles out Benny Benjamin's drumming as the key to its success: "Man, he was one of the major forces in the Motown sound. Benny could've very well been the baddest. He was the [Bernard] Purdie of the sixties. But unknown. Because for the most part these cats'd be in the studios all day, and as musicians they weren't getting that recognition then. People weren't interested in the musicians.

"Benny'd be late for sessions, Benny'd be

Above: *Stevie (kneeling, center) joins the other big name Motown groups of the time for a 1965 photocall.*

Right: *Stevie appearing on the influential UK TV pop show "Ready, Steady, Go".*

drunk sometimes. I mean, he was a beautiful cat, but . . . Benny would come up with these stories, like 'Man, you'd never believe it, but like a goddam *elephant*, man, in the middle of the road, stopped me from comin' to the session, so that's why I'm late, baby, so it's cool.' But he was *ready*. He could play drums, you wouldn't even need a bass, that's how bad he was. Just listen to all that Motown shit, like *I Can't Help Myself* and *My World Is Empty Without You* and *This Old Heart Of Mine* and *Don't Mess With Bill, Girl's Alright With Me* – the drums would just *pop*!"

Uptight elbowed aside the Beatles and Rolling Stones long enough to establish Stevie Wonder once and for all, reaching No. 3 overall and No. 1 on the R & B chart. Stevie had proved he was not a one-hit wonder – what's more, he proved he could make hits in the studio. He had carved out a niche for himself, and for the first time was really able to exercise control over his musical direction.

"If I had a tune that I dug, I did it," he says. "This is after *Uptight*, that's when I started doin' more things myself. If I had a tune, like I did *Mr. Tambourine Man*, Clarence Paul and I used to work out a lot of things because we sang a lot together. We did *Blowin' In The Wind*, and before that *Funny How Time Slips Away* used to be our closing tune, but when that got old we started to pick up on *Blowin' In The Wind*. So basically, whenever I did have a tune I wanted to do I usually did it, but I was still in school then, too, so it was kind of hard for me to get that closely involved in it. If I had a tune that I wanted them to hear, I would bring it in, tell them what key I wanted to do it in and work out the arrangements we would put it in. The first three or four albums I did mostly their suggestions, but after that I was available more of the time to work with the producer."

Motown rushed Stevie back into the studio to record a follow-up to *Uptight*. Once again Sylvia Moy and producer Henry Cosby helped write the tune, this time with co-producer William Stevenson, and they reproduced the basic idea of *Uptight* beautifully, using a simple tempo, the same cracking drum/bass pattern, another blasting brass theme and more elaborate backing vocals mixed in with Stevie's lead. The song was called *Nothing's Too Good For My Baby*. The echoes of a Bo Diddley riff lurking beneath the entire proceedings gave an added twist of ex-

citement to what was by any account a great song.

The rest of 1966 saw an explosion of material from Stevie that more than made up for his silence through most of 1965. On 4 May, the "Uptight" LP came out, a collection of hits, B-sides and fillers hooked around the title track and *Nothing's Too Good For My Baby*. *Love A Go-Go* is strongly reminiscent of Martha and the Vandellas' *Dancing In The Street*, especially on the opening theme, but with a softer feeling to the verses. *Hold Me* is a medium tempo, Sam Cooke-like ballad written by Stevie with Clarence Paul. The version of *Blowin' In The Wind* is taken pretty much straight from the live performances, with Clarence Paul sharing the vocal in a much more dramatic reading than Bob Dylan gave the song, perhaps reflecting the experiences of Stevie and his Motown colleagues in the fight against prejudice. *Teach Me Tonight* is another medium-tempo ballad with Stevie sharing the vocal and some great saxophone fills thrown in for good measure.

Stevie tries a more experimental vocal on *Ain't That Asking For Trouble*, a collaboration between himself, Clarence Paul and Sylvia Moy. Like most of the material from this era, the backing track is superb. *I Want My Baby Back* is an undiscovered Motown classic hooked around James Jamerson's monumental bass line, a track that just won't quit as Stevie skates through his vocal with the greatest of ease. This could just as easily have been a hit for the Four Tops.

Stevie's pop sensibility comes out in *Pretty Little Angel*, which sounds like a Neil Sedaka tune and is one of the less appealing songs on the record, even though Stevie co-wrote it. *Music Talk*, a slow, funky blues written by Stevie with Ted Hull, was an adequate B-side for *High Heel Sneakers*, with Stevie pitching a bizarre harp solo against brass. On this track, and on the thrown-in *Contract On Love*, Stevie's voice is pitched higher than on the rest of the record. The album finishes with a straight ballad, *With A Child's Heart*, reminiscent of the standard ballads Motown had previously made Stevie record, but with a very tasteful arrangement and a beautiful vocal reading from Stevie.

1966 was a big year for Stevie in England as well. *Uptight* was released there early in the year and Stevie did a brief promotional tour in support of the record, which was the first Stevie

Wonder single to hit the charts in England, making it as far as the top twenty.

Perhaps the most significant step Stevie took in 1966, however, was to make his first political statements on record. This was definitely against Motown's usual grain, but Stevie was flushed with the idealism of the time. In insisting on recording Bob Dylan's anti-war song *Blowin' In The Wind*, Stevie was obviously beginning to assert himself in a more thoughtful direction. He told the decidedly apolitical *Teenset* Magazine, "I'm glad I'm blind. I can see more of life this way."

Amazingly, *Blowing In The Wind* went to the top ten in America, Number One on the R&B charts (the third time Stevie had been so honored) and into the top thirty on Britain's *Music Week* charts. He continued to write his own material, turning out song after song with Cosby and Moy. *My Cherie Amour* was written during this time although Motown held it for several years before releasing it.

"I usually had things worked out," Stevie recalls. "What would happen is, Henry Cosby would do some writing with us, he would come up with a chord pattern for my melody, then maybe he'd help Sylvia Moy with the lyrics to the tune. Sylvia did a lot of writing on the early

things. I would come up with the basic idea, maybe a punch line, and she would write the story. I would give her a tape of it — I write so many tunes in bits that I really don't get the time to finish them all up, so I just give 'em to someone to do. Usually I'll write the music and basic idea for the story. Then there are times when I'm so interested in getting down to writing another tune that I give it to someone else to finish up, or I feel that my story isn't strong enough, so I give the song to Sylvia or whoever to finish up."

Steve's next single, *A Place In The Sun*, takes up where the sentiment of *Blowin' In The Wind* leaves off. The careworn optimism of the song's message and refrain in the chorus to keep "movin' on" fit neatly into the protest music sensibility of the time and could have easily applied to the civil rights movement. The song's string arrangement fits the emotional tone perfectly, and Steve's vocal is very convincing.

Despite being yet another departure from the formula that had produced Stevie's previous hits, *A Place In The Sun* did extremely well and led off his next album, "Down To Earth", which came out in the U.S. on 16 November, 1966. The record showed Stevie influenced not just by Bob Dylan but by the Beatles, especially the Paul

Stevie with the Temptations when they appeared on the same program of "Ready, Steady, Go".

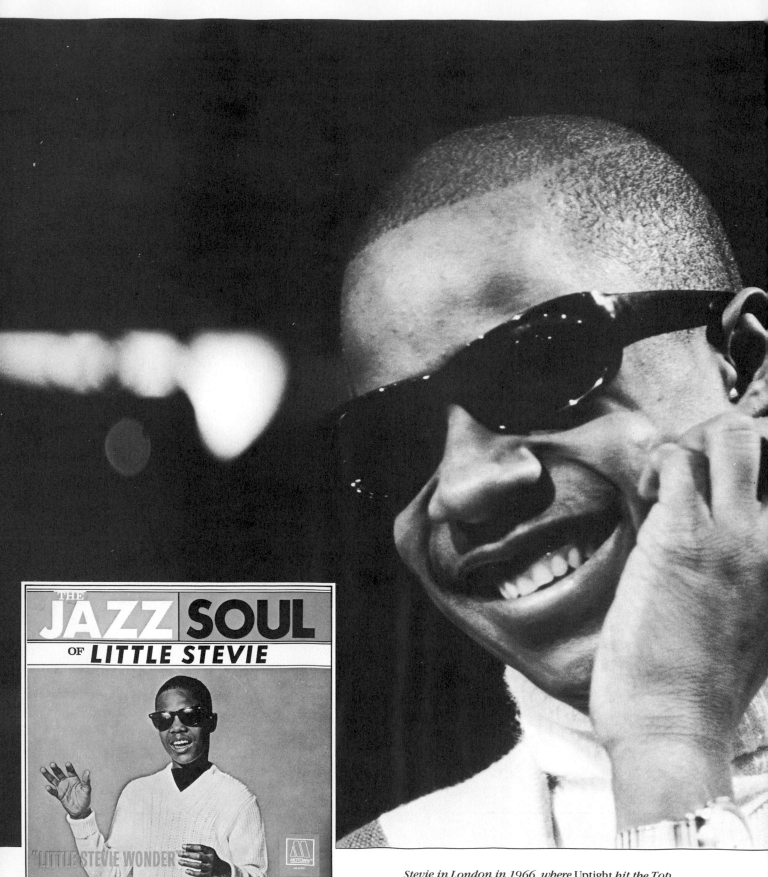

Stevie in London in 1966, where Uptight *hit the Top Twenty of the UK charts in February.*

54

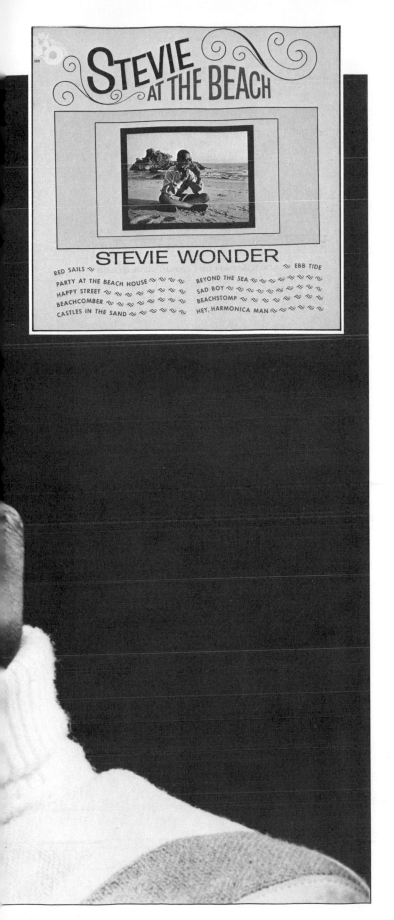

McCartney of "Rubber Soul". Like Stevie, McCartney moved easily from tender ballad sentiment to flat out rock 'n' roll. The "Rubber Soul" connection can be heard in Stevie's attempt to establish himself in a softer, lyrical mode without resorting to the Tin Pan Alley standards Motown had always made him record.

Down To Earth and *Thank You Love* are great pop R&B ballads, but *Sylvia* is a bit too cloying and *Bang Bang*, which had been a hit for Sonny and Cher, is just a bad idea. *Be Cool, Be Calm (And Keep Yourself Together)*, another Cosby/Wonder/Moy composition, rocks out spiritedly. Stevie includes a tribute to the Supremes with a fairly straight rendition of *My World Is Empty Without You*.

That Lonesome Road is a ballad similar in feel to *Blowing' In The Wind*, while *Mr. Tambourine Man* is a beautiful, Byrds-influenced rendition of the Dylan tune. *Hey Love* is a pretty pop ballad, *Angel Baby* is a hot *Uptight* remake with lots of breathless vocal pyrotechnics from Stevie, and *Sixteen Tons* is a great performance of this bluesy standard.

"Down To Earth" yielded the next few single releases. *Sylvia* On 24 October, 1966; the title track and *Thank You Love* on 16 November of the same year; and *Hey Love* on 9 February, 1967. The flip side, *Travellin' Man*, continued in the soft, melodic style that Stevie had been working on. Clarence Paul produced the track with a lush yet understated vocal/string arrangement.

The easy listening groove into which Stevie had settled culminated with the release of the sweet ballad *Until You Come Back To Me (That's What I'm Gonna Do)* on 1 May, 1967 in the U.K. only. It wasn't until the mid-seventies "Looking Back" compilation that the record was issued in the U.S., though Aretha Franklin had a big 1973 hit with the song which went to No. 3 in the U.S. charts. Stevie wrote the song with Morris Broadnax and producer Clarence Paul. His amazingly expressive voice had become by this time one of the finest ballad mediums of the modern era, a fact which would soon impress and influence old time crooners like Frank Sinatra and newcomers like Barbra Streisand. Stevie's potential was growing at an astonishing rate — at the age of seventeen he had equalled or surpassed virtually all of his competition. And he was only warming up.

7. Love Is All You Need

Few musicians took the cultural revolution that occurred in the United States and most of the world during 1967 more seriously than Stevie Wonder. His innate musical talents had been honed to a peak, and Stevie was madly soaking up influences from as many outside sources as he could listen to. Jazz, country, blues, Tin Pan Alley ballad standards and rock songwriting had all influenced him up to that point, but now the new technology associated with hard rock and funk instrumental performances came to his attention via the music of the Beatles, Rolling Stones, Jimi Hendrix, the Who and Sly and the Family Stone.

The Beatles were a continuing influence, and their landmark album, "Sgt. Pepper's Lonely Hearts Club Band", affected him just as it changed the way the world listened to music in the so-called Summer of Love. "I just dug more the effects they got," he later said, "Like echoes and voice things, the writing, like *For The Benefit Of Mr. Kite.*"

Like a lot of other young people, Stevie also experimented with drugs, but his natural state was so enhanced that drugs freaked him out: "I smoked grass one time and it scared me to death. Things just got larger. It was something new and different, but I found I'm so busy checking things out all the time anyway that I don't really need it."

Still, at the time he professed a fascination with acid rock, and later singled out Cream as a group he admired. "Some of that psychedelic music is really fantastic," he told *Melody Maker* in 1967. "It shows the creativeness of young people. I believe that music is bringing younger people closer together. Young people are expressing themselves through music, and that's bringing countries closer together."

Stevie's idealism was characteristic of the spirit of the times. His blindness enhanced the determination to go beyond surface discrimination and emphasize qualities all people shared in common. "People ask me what soul is," he explained, "but all people have soul. Soul is what you feel. So anybody can have soul and you can call it whatever you want. Psychedelic music has got soul because the people have got soul."

The musical synthesis of folk, rock, soul and jazz styles that Stevie envisaged worked its way through the course of his next album, "I Was Made To Love Her". This is the first of Stevie's great LPs, a non-stop rhythmic assault in which even the filler works inexorably toward an overall effect. The soul music explosion that was cresting not just with Motown's artists but with Wilson Pickett, Aretha Franklin, Otis Redding, James Brown and others, gave him a guideline for incorporating rock energy into R&B performance, and "I Was Made To Love Her" is fired by that energy from start to finish.

Stevie's cover of *Respect* typifies the album's strengths. The Otis Redding song which also inspired a great interpretation by Aretha Franklin is tackled by Stevie in a totally direct style, the simplest of rhythmic accompaniment phrasing his cool, Ray Charles-like delivery of the vocal and casual harmonica dance. *My Girl*, like most Motown remakes, gets an absolutely reverential treatment with respect to the original arrangement, the only embellishments being in the isolation of the string track and minor production effects against Stevie's smooth delivery.

On *Send Me Some Lovin'* and *Everybody Needs Somebody (I Need You)*, Stevie handles medium tempo soul ballads with a new-found sophistication. The latter, a smooth pop gem written by Stevie with Clarence Paul and Morris Broadnax, shouldn't be confused with the Solomon Burke rave-up *Everybody Needs Somebody To Love*. Stevie's tune is a carefully constructed single more in line with what pop/R&B groups like the Foundations were doing at the time.

Nothing shows off Stevie's sense of himself better on this record than his versions of the Holland/Dozier/Holland songs *Baby Don't Do It*

The Fool. His previous efforts in this direction were limited to the "Tribute To Uncle Ray" material, and at that point neither his voice nor his personality were particularly well suited to it. But Stevie at seventeen is a different story, and his reading of the material seems to come from the same source that inspired so many young whites, especially in England, to adopt the blues form as the perfect rock-related musical expression at around the same time. _I Pity The Fool_ is an emotion-packed vehicle for Stevie, with a pronounced guitar accompaniment and a backing-track that Stevie seems to wind up, line by line, like a mechanical toy.

The tribute to James Brown, _Please, Please, Please_, is a bit too precise to be called precocious, but Brown, particularly in this era of his work, is almost impossible to top in a cover version, and Stevie wisely decides to pay his respects rather than take him head on.

Every Time I See You I Go Wild is the album's Motown production number, setting a Supremes-like treatment to the arrangement, and Stevie rocks it for all he's worth. _I'd Cry_, the hard-rocking single that had been previously released, is carried forward to fill out this collection.

The triumph of the set, though, is the title track, a tune written by Stevie for his girlfriend, Angie. The intro itself is magnificent. The bass and a distorted guitar (or electric sitar) plunk out the sprightly theme in unison with strings swelling on the overtones and Stevie's harmonica, laying down a sweet melody before he charges into the vocal. His singing is possessed, and James Jamerson does hoop tricks around his voice with a spectacular bass line while Benny Benjamin pushes a subtle snare drum pattern underneath. Stevie keeps a cyclical intensity to his delivery, winding up breathlessly at each line's end. Then the beat shifts into a shuffle and the tambourines choogle in while Stevie just keeps pushing, throwing in chorus after joyful chorus.

I Was Made To Love Her brought Stevie new heights of success, not just in the US, but worldwide. He was riding the crest, and he knew it. "I wrote _I Was Made To Love Her_ in about ten minutes," he boasted.

Flushed with his young love, continuing success and late-sixties optimism, Steve performed brilliantly during his 1967 British tour despite a

and _Can I Get A Witness_. Stevie has often been critical of the inflexibility of Holland/Dozier/Holland material, which he maintains was largely responsible for much of the sameness of the Motown sound, but he charges these songs with the force of his personality. The rocking, weaving vocal on _Can I Get A Witness_ is a brilliant adaptation of the song's gospel character, while his _Baby Don't You Do It_ swings the song out of its lock-step convention, and when he pushes into double-time, raising the register of his voice to pitch the excitement, he remakes the song in his image. No other Motown singer ever managed to destroy the boundaries of one of the tunes written inside the organization in the way that Stevie did here.

Stevie shows a new-found mastery over the slow blues form with _A Fool For You_ and _I Pity_

throat infection that severely limited the range and power of his vocals. Wonder was full of self confidence, as he told *Melody Maker*: "I'm thankful to God because I've had a chance to understand much younger and therefore plan my life much sooner. I go to places like London and Paris and it's just fantastic understanding people and atmospheres. They help me to write songs, too."

But for all of Stevie's optimism, there were dark clouds on the horizon. The advancements in civil rights and the developing sense of a new era of cooperation between young people and minorities in the United States was counterbalanced by increasing racial hatred from older whites unwilling to accept the end of segregation and a brutal assassination conspiracy that took the lives of some of the decade's most powerful cultural leaders – John F. Kennedy, Malcolm X and before long the Rev. Martin Luther King and Robert Kennedy. Stevie was experiencing the exhilaration of being part of the "love generation" in 1967 when he went to "Swinging London", but back home in Detroit, 1967 would not be remembered as a summer of love at all.

In the early hours of Sunday morning, 23 July, a party raged at the offices of the United Civic League for Community Action on Twelfth Street in Detroit. The place was a "blind pig", an illegal after-hours bar, and it was packed with late night drinkers. Stevie Wonder's *I Was Made To Love Her* blasted out of a juke box stocked with Motown singles.

At 3.45 am, plain-clothes patrolman Charles Henry entered the club and ordered a beer. Fifteen minutes later four cops raided the joint, breaking down the door with sledgehammers, and arrested the 80 or so patrons on hand. It took police 45 minutes to ferry the bar's clientele to the police station in squad cars, long enough to attract a large, angry mob. As the last prisoners were taken into custody someone threw a bottle at a police car, shattering its rear window.

The Detroit riots of 1967 had begun. Throughout the night, looters declared open house on the stores along Twelfth Street. The next day looting intensified, and an estimated crowd of 3,000 people pelted police and firemen with rocks and bottles. By Sunday night Twelfth Street was an avenue of burning build-

ings. Krikor Messerlian, an immigrant shoemaker, became the first casualty of the riots when he tried to protect his business with a saber and was clubbed to death in the street by looters, in full view of many witnesses.

As the looting and burning spread to other sections of the city, the National Guard was called in. Police reported a number of sniper attacks from rooftops, but in the chaotic situation private citizens, merchants and security guards were all firing their guns at will. Total anarchy prevailed. After another full day of riots, President Lyndon Johnson announced that he was sending federal troops to Detroit to quell the disturbance.

The city was literally a war zone. On Tuesday, over 1,000 people were arrested on a variety of charges, people were shot on sight by police merely for being on the street, and snipers had

Above: *Stevie Wonder deserved the congratulations of his colleagues at Motown when* I Was Made To Love Her *reached the Top Ten in both the U.S. and U.K. in 1967. Sidney Poitier looks on.*

two separate police precinct houses covered with rifle fire. A number of innocent bystanders, even people hiding in their own homes, were killed in the crossfire of fierce gun battles. At least one guardsman was killed by crossfire from his own unit.

By Thursday, 27 July, the riots had stopped – 43 people had been killed, many of them without breaking any laws, and whole sections of the city had been gutted by fire, leaving thousands of families homeless. The riots served to polarize further an already tense and divided city. The sense of abandonment in the city's black community grew even worse.

Stevie Wonder was not unaffected by these events, but instead of becoming embittered, he became more determined to spread his idealistic views. Though Gordy was adamant about keeping Motown artists out of the political arena, Stevie managed to promote his beliefs via more circuitous ways. He had written a Christmas song in 1966 called *Someday At Christmas*, which was a cleverly disguised medium for social comment. Using the idealism associated with Christmas spirit as the thematic hook, Wonder made the song a catalogue of complaints about social injustice and world political problems. Motown re-released the song at the end of 1967 as part of an album package called "Someday At Christmas", filled out with Stevie

Above: *Stevie with Junior Walker in London.* Right: *By 1967 the maturing voice of Stevie Wonder made him equally skillful at handling soulful ballads and up-tempo funkers.*

singing Yuletide standards like *Silver Bells, The Little Drummer Boy*, and *Ave Maria.*

Stevie continued his successful songwriting collaboration with Sylvia Moy and producer Henry Cosby, writing *I'm Wondering*, the excellent follow-up single to *I Was Made To Love Her*, which relied on a similar rhythmic pattern as *. . . Love Her*, and another fantastic Jamerson bass line. In March 1968 the same songwriting team returned to Stevie's more pastoral mode with *Shoo-Be-Doo-Be-Doo-Da-Day*, which featured a wonderful Muscle Shoals style rhythm section and that unforgettable chorus.

The song came too late to be included on Stevie's first Greatest Hits package, which was released the same month and featured *Uptight (Everything's Alright), I'm Wondering, I Was Made To Love Her, A Place In The Sun, Contract On Love, Fingertips Pt II*, and *Nothing's Too Good For My Baby.*

On 4 April, 1968, Dr Martin Luther King was assassinated while preparing to lead a march of striking sanitation workers in Memphis, Tennessee. The assassination ignited smoldering tempers in inner cities throughout the United States. Riots broke out in 125 American cities, including Chicago and Detroit. At the time Stevie was one of Motown's biggest artists, riding high on the success of *Shoo-Be-Doo-Be-Doo-Da-Day* and the Greatest Hits album. Though he yearned to make some kind of a statement of his philosophy in this climate, Motown was not about to let him tamper with the formula just when he was coming into his own as a popular artist. Stevie would struggle against this mold for the next two years before finally releasing his political concept album, "Where I'm Coming From", which would incorporate his views on equal rights and his opposition to the war in Viet Nam that was also dividing American society in the late sixties.

Though Motown wasn't quite ready to let Stevie become a full-time protest singer, the company definitely wanted him to keep turning out the string of hits he was amassing. Songwriting took up an increasingly large amount of Stevie's time and energy. He wrote songs with a variety of collaborators, including his mother Lula. Lula was in on a number of songwriting sessions because Stevie would have people come over to his house to write songs and Lula would cook for them, and occasionally throw in a songwriting suggestion.

"Most of the spare time I get I spend writing songs," Stevie said at the time. "Reading stimulates me to write more. If you get wrapped up in a book it stimulates you. Sometimes I write as many as 150 songs a month down in my basement at home, then I'll take them to the studio. I would like to write more and stop singing so much. I like writing even more than singing. With writing you leave something behind."

Steve's next song, *You Met Your Match*, was a lively funk-rocker which anticipated the clavinet-based singles of his later career. Written by Stevie, Lula and Don Hunter, the record failed to make an impression on the public. It took a break from such self-written material to chalk up Stevie's next major chart success.

For Once In My Life was a slickly crafted song written by Ron Miller and Orlando Murden, with an exquisite Henry Cosby arrangement that made careful use of piano and flute fills for coloration. The writers had intended it to be a show business standard, and dozens of shlock versions of the tune had been recorded before Stevie put his unmistakable stamp on it, singing through the song's original intent, charging it with passion and adding a hot harmonica solo. Miller reportedly didn't like the way Stevie recorded his song, which is ironic since it climbed to the second spot on the American singles chart and to number three in England — the highest placing Stevie had enjoyed in the U.K..

Before *For Once In My Life* was released, Berry Gordy Jr. got the weird idea of releasing an instrumental single of Stevie covering the Burt Bacharach/Hal David tune *Alfie* under the pseudonym of Eivets Rednow, which, of course, is Stevie Wonder spelled backwards. The rendition was unquestionably beautiful, but so out of character for Stevie that it was no wonder they decided to disguise his involvement, however baldly.

Alfie fared poorly as a single, yet Motown went on to release a whole album of harmonica instrumentals. Cosby's production of this material is the gaudiest stuff he ever put together for Stevie, fairly drowning him in sheets of strings and orchestral soundtrack music. A 6.45 production number of *Ruby* makes very little sense, though the inclusion of Stevie's own compositions — *Which Way The Wind, Bye Bye*

World, How Can You Believe and *More Than A Dream* – keeps the record from being a total loss. The two best moments on the record come on *Grazing In The Grass* and *More Than A Dream*, when the strings take a back seat to a crisp jazz ensemble and Stevie cuts loose with his most impassioned playing on the set.

In December of 1968 Motown released Stevie's next album, "For Once In My Life", hooked around the title track, *Shoo-Be-Doo-Be-Doo-Da-Day* and *You Met Your Match*. Those three songs combined for a powerful opening sequence to the album's first side, which continued with several more of Stevie's compositions – *I Wanna Make You Love Me*, a throwaway up-tempo love song with a catchy instrumental break, *I'm More Than Happy (I'm Satisfied)*, a smooth medium-tempo ballad, and *I*

Don't Know Why, a very powerful love song with a vocal performance obviously inspired by Otis Redding.

The second side was a typical Motown collection of standard-style material. The lead-off track was a brooding, introspective version of the great Bobby Hebb song *Sunny*, featuring a terrific harmonica solo. *I'd Be A Fool Right Now* followed, a beautiful song fired by a dynamic shuffle rhythm guided by Benjamin and Jamerson, then *Ain't No Lovin'*, which turns on a cleverly understated piano theme. Stevie gives a wonderful reading of the song most closely associated with the great Billie Holiday, *God Bless The Child*. The album closes with Stevie's own *Do I Love Her*, a lighthearted love song, and the swinging *The House On The Hill*, which was also included on "Alfie" in an instrumental

Stevie receives a congratulatory kiss from his mother Lula when he graduated from the Michigan School for the Blind in June 1969.

brilliantly in a lush, romantic setting. Motown may have felt the song came too close to sounding like McCartney, since they released it only as a B-side, but the public felt differently. When the single was released it was *My Cherie Amour* that got the caller requests and the airplay.

Before it had run its course, *My Cherie Amour* was almost as successful as *For Once In My Life*, and became the title track of Stevie's next album. Aside from this, the main focus of the record from Motown's standpoint was to follow up *For Once In My Life*. Another Ron Miller song, *Yester-Me, Yester-You, Yesterday* was included in an obvious attempt to cash in on the success of *For Once In My Life*, but the song had less of the feeling of abandon that distinguished *For Once...*, coming closer to the standard-ballad approach used by the Ray Charles Singers. Another song called *At Last* is carried by a popping bass line but uses a background arrangement almost identical to *For Once In My Life*.

Except for an attempt to update the Oscar Hammerstein/Richard Rogers standard *Hello Young Lovers*, the rest of the album is pretty much turned over to Stevie's interests. His version of *Light My Fire*, done closer to the style of Jose Feliciano than the Doors, includes some of his most inventive harmonica playing, especially the unusual (for him) technique of overdubbing harmonica accents under his own vocals. At such moments it becomes apparent how close his voice timbre matches the coloration, rhythmic inventiveness and feel of his harmonica playing. Steve gives a torchy vocal to the standard *The Shadow Of Your Smile*, while his syrupy ballad, *Angie Girl*, was culled from the flip side of *For Once In My Life* for inclusion.

Angie Girl, like virtually all of Stevie's self-penned love songs at this time, was written for his first girlfriend Angie. Lyricist Sylvia Moy often changed the name in some songs or simply omitted naming the girl to prevent all of Stevie's material from having a title based around "Angie". *Give Your Love*, a stark, impressive love song written by Stevie with Don Hunter and Henry Cosby, features a spoken intro (and once again refers to Angie).

You And Me is probably the best arrangement on the record, an absolutely irresistible rhythm track matched with perfectly aligned voice and

version, and is distinguished here by some excellent bass and guitar accompaniment.

1969 would be a year of great changes for Stevie. He finished his "formal" education upon his graduation from the Michigan School for the Blind, and his lessons with Ted Hull also ended. He became even more active in promoting his career, and toured extensively.

Motown released Stevie's fantastic *I Don't Know Why* from "For Once In My Life" as his next single in January, 1969. The flip side was a song he'd written a few years before when he first became influenced by Paul McCartney's songwriting with the Beatles. "Rubber Soul", the Beatles' transitional album, featured McCartney's classic ballad, the French/English *Michelle*, and *My Cherie Amour* uses the same approach

Above left: Stevie Wonder meets President Nixon in the Rose Garden at the White House, where he came on 5 May 1969 to receive the Distinguished Service Award from the

64

string parts and two harmonica solos. Another fantastic Jamerson bass riff blows *Pearl* into orbit as Stevie's inspired vocal is once again contrasted by an inventive backing vocal chorus, this time by a male trio.

Stevie's other songs on the album show him opening up conceptually. *I've Got You*, written with only Sylvia Moy's help on lyrics, is a clever pop tune with an interesting arrangement twist, as the theme is stated in bleating staccato delivery instead of the smooth, legato lines characteristic of most Motown arrangements. *Somebody Knows, Somebody Cares*, written with Lula, Sylvia and Cosby, heads in an outright rock direction, with a particularly dirty sounding harmonica part completely unlike Stevie's usual style.

In March Stevie returned to England for a two week, nationwide tour, opening to an enthusiastic capacity crowd at the Hammersmith Odeon in London. Appearing with Stevie were the Foundations and the Flirtations. "This is about my fifth trip here," he told *Melody Maker*. "I'm almost a native of England. I like the people here very much, they're so relaxed."

Wonder's live shows really began to take off during the summer of '69. In June he headlined a soul variety revue at the Apollo Theater in New York, then later in the summer he co-headlined the Harlem Cultural Festival, a large outdoor show, with Sly and the Family Stone. This was only a matter of weeks before Sly's legendary appearance at the Woodstock Festival, where he made such an impression on the 500,000-strong, mostly-white crowd that his career skyrocketed. One can only speculate what effect Stevie might have had on that Woodstock crowd, but he was certainly Sly's match on that summer afternoon.

Stevie was bursting away from the Vegas-style set-up that Motown sent him out with, including an orchestra led by Gene Kees. The power-packed version of *Shoo-Be-Doo-Be...* was so much faster and funkier than the recorded version that the crowd could hardly believe it. Though it would be two years before Stevie would make his official break from Motown's strategies, his clavinet playing on *Shoo-Be-Doo-Be...* sounds like the missing link between his Motown-controlled style and the progressive breakthrough that would later produce such classics as *Superstition*.

Late in 1969 Stevie's *Yester-Me, Yester-You,*

President's Committee on the Employment of the Handicapped.

Yesterday was released and eventually hit the top ten in both the U.S. and England. Though it was ostensibly a love song, it could also have been read as a song about the end of an era. 1969 had seen the beautiful spirit of Woodstock turn into ugliness at Altamont. It was a year that also saw the Beatles break up; Motown too had changed. Diana Ross left the Supremes to pursue her own career. She was replaced by Jean Terrell. Martha and the Vandellas were forced to stop touring due to illness. One of the key elements of the Motown sound disappeared forever when drummer Benny Benjamin died in an automobile accident. The era and the company that had nurtured Stevie had changed, but Stevie was ready. The boy wonder was about to come of age.

8. Steveland Hits Stride

By the age of twenty, Stevie Wonder had begun to exercise real control over both his music and his personal life. He had always been sure of his talent, but had been meticulously cared for and guided since he was eleven years old. Motown raised Stevie; the company gave him a break he could never have gotten anywhere else — it gave him the opportunity to put hands on the instruments of his expression, to learn to use recording facilities, to learn writing and arrangement. The company stuck with him and encouraged him even after his first efforts failed to crack the market, even when it seemed he might have only had a single hit with *Fingertips Part II*.

But Motown's concentration on hit singles and its caution about allowing individual artists too much freedom worked against Stevie Wonder as he matured into a more visionary musician. Though the family nurtured him at first, the organization stifled him as he grew. An indication of the stylistic dilemma with which Stevie was presented is shown in the difference between his performance on the 1969 recording "Motown Revue Live", which included high powered renditions of *For Once In My Life*, *Shoo-Be-Do-Be...* and *Uptight*; and "Stevie Wonder Live", the cabaret-like presentation from the same era, a lounge set with numbers like *I Gotta Be Me*, *Love Theme From Romeo And Juliet* and *By The Time I Get To Phoenix*.

The depth of Motown's misunderstanding of Stevie's true musical direction is evident in a 1969 interview with Stevie's musical director Gene Kees (who had taken over from Clarence Paul in 1967): "By the time he's 21," Kee said, "he will have become Stevie Wonder the entertainer, not just Stevie Wonder the maker of pop records. He has the potential to be another Sammy Davis."

It would be hard to think of a more inappropriate comparison to make, but the remark is in keeping with the way Motown viewed the music business. Motown acts were groomed to play Las Vegas night clubs, not rock concert halls. Kee:

"Tamla has a complete service for their artists. The artist development people look after everything from buying their clothes to getting them to the job on time. You have to select material for the artist, cut the act and sharpen it up, depending on where they are playing, check choreography and generally act objectively for the artist."

Such objectivity was far from Stevie's interest. Though he was fairly careful in his remarks about the company, Stevie clearly did not agree with its objectives. "I think the Tamla sound is gradually changing," he said somewhat hopefully in one interview. "Have you heard the Temptations' *Cloud Nine*? It's more or less what we call funkadelic. It's a combination of R&B, psychedelic and funky African-type beat. I'm experimenting. A lot of things I've done recently are funkadelic."

Whatever he chose to call it, Stevie was in the process of assembling his first masterpiece, one of the finest records made in a year of high quality music, "Signed, Sealed And Delivered". Though the songs weren't written and recorded as a unit intended for an album package, they nevertheless offered a coherent form when taken together, casting an altogether new light on Stevie's musical personality.

The plaintive, secular gospel world-weariness of *Never Had A Dream Come True* is an altogether new feeling for Stevie, and though the song, which was released as a single in early 1970, didn't fare especially well commercially, it marked a turning point in his musical approach. Henry Cosby, who co-wrote it with Stevie and Sylvia Moy, is still listed as producer, but Stevie certainly put more into the creative decisions, and the new-found emotional depth of his voice is well accompanied by the subtle, intelligent inter-relationship of the instruments in the arrangement. Even the characteristic Motown strings are on their best behavior here, enhancing the overall feel but never intruding, sharing a symbiotic relationship with the stately fuzz

guitar line which frames the tune.

On Stevie's version of the Lennon/McCartney chestnut *We Can Work It Out* we hear completely new sound. Paul McCartney's first solo album had featured the by-then ex-Beatle playing all the instruments himself, and Stevie was not to be outdone on his Beatles tribute, producing, arranging and playing all the parts on the song. This is an incredible piece of music, completely unlike anything else produced by Motown at this point, a message that rings out from the first distorted Fender Rhodes electric piano notes, framed in emulation of the Beatles' recording sound on the record known as The White Album ("The Beatles"). The crisp Motown rhythm section is missing (gone forever, in fact, since the death of drummer Benny Benjamin), replaced by a booming, muddy, McCartney-like bass sound and Stevie's distinctively slogging drum style.

The truly remarkable aspect of Stevie's one-man-band approach to making this song is in the vocals. The main lines are sung in a swinging, soulful delivery, but Stevie overdubs half a dozen new vocal characters as choral elements — low, deep-throated "heys" at the end of one phrase alternating with high pitched ones at the end of the next phrase. Stevie's uncanny sense of metric counterpoint uses these elements to balance the funky equation he twists through the song.

Stevie sings both the Lennon and McCartney parts in overdubbed harmony on the chorus, recreating them perfectly without copying the actual sound of their voices and makes simultaneous reference to the chorus of the original in the overtones of the bass/piano backing. Stevie writes a new vocal arrangement for the harmonica break, slashing one knife-edge high note against the solo four times, twice in staccato, holding the next note while dropping it a step to sing the title. Over the next verse he adds a scat vocal of "baby, baby" with polarized accents on the syllables, then runs all these vocals simultaneously into a climactic finale.

This is the work of an analytical genius and McCartney must have gone bonkers when he heard it! Ditto Berry Gordy Jr., though maybe not for the same reason.

The opening electric sitar statement of *Signed, Sealed, Delivered (I'm Yours)* segues perfectly from the fading image of *We Can Work*

Left: *At twenty, Stevie's new sophistication made itself known in the brilliant LP entitled "Signed, Sealed And Delivered". Right: Motown's publicity shots in 1970 emphasized Stevie's talents as an "all-round entertainer".*

It Out. The descending theme breaks to a short cry from Stevie, then to his joyous vocal battle with honking baritone saxophone grunts, swelling trumpets and ethereal girl-group background singing. The interplay between Steve and the backing vocalists is an exquisitely personal exchange with call-and-response screams and awesome harmonic inventiveness.

The enthusiasm that charges Stevie's delivery on *Signed, Sealed, Delivered (I'm Yours)* was due in part to the songwriting collaboration it christened. Stevie wrote it with his mother, Lee Garrett and Syreeta Wright. Garrett met Stevie in Philadelphia during one of the early Motown tours and the two became fast friends. Blind since birth, Garrett had moved to Philadelphia in 1963 and gravitated to the music scene in that city. "I spent most of two years hanging out at the Uptown Theater," he recalls. "I'd watch all the rock 'n' roll shows and I got to meet a lot of the performers as they'd come through town. That's how I met Stevie Wonder."

Garrett shared Stevie's sense of humor and his love for practical jokes. Since he was a blind, black musician a few people had already confused him with Stevie Wonder and the two played this confusion to the hilt — Steve once dragged Garrett on-stage at a show and introduced him as "Stevie Wonder". Garrett also used to defy Ted Hull's curfews for Stevie. "They used to put Stevie to bed at night," he says, "and I'd go wake him up and get him out of bed; the two of us would go out cruisin' around the town at 4 am."

Garrett later became a Philadelphia disc jockey, then moved in 1967 to Detroit's WGPR-FM, where he renewed his friendship with Stevie. While he was looking for an apartment in the city, Stevie invited Garrett to stay at his family's place.

Syreeta Wright was a secretary at Motown who aspired to be a singer. This was not an unprecedented route — Martha Reeves had worked as a secretary for the company before getting the chance to substitute for Mary Wells on a session, thus launching her singing career. Stevie liked Syreeta, and when he started producing groups for Motown on an experimental basis he cut a side with her under the pseudonym Rita Wright. Garrett kidded Stevie about his fondness for Syreeta, and they came up with the punchline, *Signed, Sealed, Delivered*. Stevie asked Syreeta to come to his place for a song-writing session with Lee and Lula and come up with some words to the song.

Signed, Sealed, Delivered (I'm Yours) was a smash hit, which along with a song written by the same collaborators, *It's A Shame* (which was a gold record for the Spinners in 1970), established Stevie's production credentials.

Heaven Help Us All, which follows the title track on the "Signed, Sealed And Delivered" album, and was released as a single later in 1970, was another Ron Miller composition. This time Miller was totally attuned to Stevie's sensibility, writing a moving gospel lament cataloging the tribulations of a series of lost souls. In the song's most dramatic moment, Stevie sings "Heaven help the roses when the bombs begin to fall", a line that really gave voice to his own sentiment.

A funk rhythm pattern, stuttering clavinet accompaniment, new lyrics and a grunting vocal are the embellishments Stevie adds with Henry Cosby and Sylvia Moy to the traditional folk blues *You Can't Judge A Book By Its Cover*.

Above left: *Stevie Wonder with two young patients from the Eye Institute of the Columbia Presbyterian Medical Center in New York in March 1970. He often made*

Where Bo Diddley used the tune as a sexual boast ("I may look like a farmer but I'm a lover") in the version credited to Willie Dixon, Stevie's rendition makes the title a maxim about the complexities of love. Though Stevie tells his lover, "You're warmer than July", he goes on to warn her "I can't let you know you're getting to me". The sassy vocal group responds to him in appropriately teasing and scolding tones.

The final track on side one of "Signed, Sealed And Delivered" continues the musical tour de force. A gospel piano intro heralds *Sugar*, which Stevie starts out at a medium tempo and gradually builds to tremendous intensity, cutting an outstanding guitar solo from one of the Motown session players through verse after verse of his vocal.

Side Two of the album opens with the romantic ballads *I Wonder Why* and *Anything You Want Me To Do*, then builds to the dramatic plea *I Can't Let My Heaven Walk Away*, before returning to the funk factory for *Joy (Takes Over Me)*.

I Gotta Have A Song is one of Steve's finest compositions. Once again the premise of the song is tragic, in this case lost love, but with a marvelous emotional twist, Stevie holds out hope through music. When all the losses cataloged in each verse mount up, the chorus explodes into optimistic redemption: "Show me to where there's music." Music makes life worth living, Stevie is saying in this tribute to the sustaining spiritual powers of aesthetic beauty. When things go wrong, "I gotta have a song."

The album closes with a simple love song, *Something To Say*, in which Stevie urges his new love to have faith in their relationship despite the possible adversities listed in the song. In its confidence in the power of love to overcome the problems of the world, the song looks forward to the next recorded project Stevie would attempt – his first concept album, "Where I'm Coming From".

Stevie really believed that his demonstrable love of humanity made a difference. In March 1970 Stevie made a surprise visit to the children's ward at Columbia Presbyterian Medical Center in New York, a hospital that aided under-privileged children. Stevie would go on to make impromptu and often unpublicized visits to hospitals and charitable orgnizations.

His relationship with Syreeta Wright, which

had become a subtext of some of his writing, had also flowered during 1970. On 30 June they announced their engagement in London. Syreeta, who was a transcendental meditation teacher, encouraged Steve to delve into eastern philosophy and mysticism.

On 14 September Steve and Syreeta married at the Burnette Baptist Church in Detroit. Upon their return from a Bermuda honeymoon Stevie and Syreeta began work on the album concept he'd been wanting to make for a long time.

"Where I'm Coming From" would be the last product Stevie delivered to Motown under the terms of his original agreement with the company. His dissatisfaction with the way Motown worked and his own role in the organization had reached a peak. "I was in the process of getting my thing together," he says, "and deciding what I was gonna do with my life." He enjoyed producing, but despite the fact that he had produced gold records with *Signed, Sealed, Delivered (I'm Yours)* and *It's A Shame* (for the

unannounced visits to schools and hospitals. Above right: *Stevie announced his engagement to Syreeta Wright on a visit to London in July 1970.*

Spinners), he felt that Motown was not particularly interested in his ideas. When he produced a follow-up to *It's A Shame* for the Spinners, *We'll Have It Made*, the song went nowhere, and Stevie felt that the company just wasn't behind it. "I wanted that tune to be big," he says. "I was so hurt when it didn't do it."

Other songs Stevie produced, including one with Martha Reeves, weren't even released. "I was 20 going on 21 and so a lot of things were left somewhat un-followed-up by me. I would get the product there and nobody would listen to it and I'd say, 'Fuckit' ... I wouldn't worry about it."

The only thing for Stevie to do was insist on total creative control of his album project, a concession hard won from Gordy, who prided himself in keeping tabs on every piece of work produced by his company. Nevertheless, Gordy was mindful of the fact that Stevie was dissatisfied with his treatment at Motown, and with an important contract renewal in the offing, Stevie was given the go-ahead to make the album without any outside interference from the company.

Stevie and Syreeta worked for the better part of a year on the material for "Where I'm Coming From". The record reflected the musical in-

Above left: *Syreeta and Stevie cutting their wedding cake at the reception given for them in Detroit by Motown Records after their marriage on 14 September 1970.*

fluences Stevie had been cultivating — Jimi Hendrix, Roland Kirk, Sly Stone, Eric Clapton — and was the most strident, bitter collection of lyrics he ever assembled, reflecting his disillusion with Motown and with an American political system that left liberal leaders like the Kennedy brothers, Malcolm X and Martin Luther King dead from assassins' bullets and put the devious and eventually criminal Richard M. Nixon in office to preside over the Viet Nam war.

Stevie's sympathy with American soldiers killed in a war he felt the country shouldn't have been fighting was a between-the-lines message throughout the record, and the metaphorical subject matter of *Think Of Me As Your Soldier*, one of the songs from the album. "Sometimes I wish that I could have been all the soldiers that were killed in Viet Nam," he said. "I guess you could call it a sacrificial wish."

Stevie points an accusing finger at the older generation (which he felt had ducked its responsibilities) on *I Wanna Talk To You*, a bitter dialog between two people on opposite sides of the generation gap who eventually suffer from a communications breakdown. It's tempting to view this song as Stevie's ultimate complaint against the value system upheld by Motown. The lengthy lament *Sunshine In Their Eyes* offers Stevie another platform to condemn society's acceptance of social injustice.

On *Do Yourself A Favor*, a funk process track with a decidedly "live" feel that blasts out a non-stop groove for nearly six minutes, Steve warns listeners to "educate your mind", in between percussive stabs from clavinet and Hammond-B-3 organ and countless layers of syncopated vocal overlays.

Even at his bleakest moments, though, Steve never presents a world view completely devoid of hope. For all of the social criticism in "Where I'm Coming From", the record still leaves plenty of room for redemption through love. *Take Up A Course In Happiness* and *Something Out Of The Blue* are characteristic Stevie Wonder love songs, the latter riding a soft guitar and flute backing with a very smooth touch.

If You Really Love Me, the album's only hit single, shows that Steve was keeping tabs on the current commercial mood. The opening section of the song is an arrangement straight out of the Blood Sweat and Tears/Chicago style, which is contrasted with a slower tempo segment in an A-B-A-B-A pattern throughout the song.

Never Dreamed You'd Leave In Summer offers an elegaic side to Steve's love ballads, a wistful acceptance of lost love that adds depth to his previous emotional consideration of the subject, and anticipates the way he would go on to transform personal statements about his love life into universal love songs.

"Where I'm Coming From" was not especially well accepted as an album, and it yielded fewer hit singles than Stevie's other recent records, but it was the first time Stevie had used the LP format as a complete medium for self-expression. The music and the songwriting on "Where I'm Coming From" formed Stevie's personal statement about life in the late sixties. He is proud of the record, even for its flaws, and maintains that it would have been far more successful if Motown had understood it better.

"I don't think it was promoted properly," he says. 'Where I'm Coming From' was kinda premature to some extent, but I wanted to express myself. A lot of it now I'd probably remix."

Obviously, the need for self-expression outweighed any other considerations for Stevie, who realized that he could do no worse with his own ideas than Motown had done by forcing him to record so many hack standards. Stevie was about to take the situation into his own hands and rely on his own ideas.

Above right: *Leaving the wedding reception. Syreeta was an aspiring singer who also taught transcendental meditation.*

9. Breakaway

On 13 May, 1971, Stevie Wonder became 21 years old. Overnight he went from being almost totally controlled by the Motown organization to having full determination over his own destiny. His childhood contract with Motown expired on his twenty-first birthday, the same day that all the money held in trust for him came due.

Stevie had planned very carefully for this moment. Ewart Abner, who was the president of Motown Records at the time, had had an inkling that Stevie was dissatisfied, for the boy had given him a warning at a meeting two years previously. "He was about nineteen then," says Abner. "He used to remind me that his day was coming, that when he turned 21 he was going to do what he wanted to do. I used to ask him – or tell him – to do things, and he'd say 'Okay, but when I'm 21 I'm going to have things my own way. I don't think you know where I'm coming from. I don't think you can understand it'."

Even with this advance warning, Abner was still unprepared for what happened when he sat down with Stevie to renegotiate a new contract. "He came to me and said 'I'm 21 now. I'm not gonna do what you say any more. Void my contract.' I freaked."

Stevie demanded that Motown pay him the money he'd earned during the course of his childhood contract. Motown forked out one million dollars. Stevie took the money and left Detroit for New York, where he hired a room at the Howard Johnson Motor Inn on the west side of Manhattan, booking time at Electric Lady studios in Greenwich Village to record his next album.

At the time Electric Lady Studios, located on Eighth Street in the heart of the Village, was the most sought after studio space in New York City. Its state-of-the-art technology and hip, relaxed ambience were the legacy of the late Jimi Hendrix to the music scene he loved so much. Hendrix had poured a vast amount of his earnings into building the studio during his lifetime and spent every spare moment he had working on song ideas, some of which have subsequently been released on posthumous Hendrix albums. Stevie Wonder, who would become as notorious as Hendrix had been for spending all his free time in the studio, was naturally drawn to this setting to make his first totally personal musical statement. He also did some recording at Media Sound in New York, and Crystal Industries in Los Angeles.

"My contract with Motown ended May 13, of 1971," says Stevie, "and I decided to just not sign with anybody for a while and just cool it. I was thinking of looking at other companies. I talked to just about every company there was.

"I had gone about as far as I could go. I wasn't growing; I just kept repeating 'The Stevie Wonder Sound', and it didn't express how I felt about what was happening in the world I decided to go for something else besides a winning formula. I wanted to see what would happen if I changed."

Stevie had a handful of songs written and partially written with this project in mind. "I decided to take all the money that had accumulated and invest it into the kind of music that I had never really been able to get into before. So I just barricaded myself with the instruments in the studio, drums, piano, clavinet.

"I isolated myself. I wanted to find the right way to express myself. I did all the parts on the album because I didn't have a group at the time. I wanted to make people *aware* of some things. Things don't get better automatically. The only way for something to get better is to check it out."

Before he had finished recording the tracks which would appear on the "Music Of My Mind" album, Stevie had spent a quarter of a million dollars on studio time alone. He all but lived in the studio for the better part of a year. The first thing he did was put down all the basic song ideas he wanted to choose from: "I recorded 40 tunes in about two weeks. They weren't totally

finished, I just did piano basics or whatever. I would just lay down what came to mind, on the piano or on the clavinet, usually one of the two instruments. Depending on the instruments the songs do come out differently, 'cause an instrument is like a color, it puts you in a certain mood."

While in New York, Stevie went to a recording session being held by Richie Havens, where he met Robert Margouleff and Malcolm Cecil, two composers and engineers who were working on the session and were experts on synthesizer technology. Stevie expressed an interest in their work, and they gave him a copy of their electronic music album, "Tonto's Expanding Head Band". Stevie was fascinated with the record and hired the two to engineer his new music and program his synthesizers.

Through Havens Stevie made another crucially important contact — music business lawyer Johannen Vigoda, who would later negotiate Steve's next contract.

Stevie had always experimented with different instruments, but the introduction of synthesizers to his conceptual package was a turning point in his recording career. Stevie had an uncanny knack with electronic instruments, coaxing an unprecedented warmth and emotional depth out of them instead of using them simply to produce gimmicky sounds, as was

most commonly the case in their early applications to music.

Though there had been no firm plan to use synthesizers, Stevie quickly adjusted to make them an integral part of his sound. "I heard some of Walter Carlos' work, and that's how I really got interested in it. I was outside a music shop somewhere, and they had a synthesizer there and I was listening to some tunes and decided that I had to get one. This was about the 28th of May, 1971. I started out just playing one tune with the synthesizer called *Home Free* and I dug it so much that I just decided to use it wherever I could."

With Margouleff and Cecil programming the functions of his synthesizers and engineering their incorporation into his recording arrangements, Stevie painstakingly worked out the character of the sounds he wanted from the instruments, spending hours and hours in the studio experimenting until he came up with the feeling he wanted.

"I think a lot of people look at a synthesizer as just another freaky instrument, but I look at it as another tool for expressing myself. The way you play an instrument has a lot to do with the character of yourself. You play in a certain way. You can really get into feeling people through their music, you can sometimes sense where you're at by how they play. It's like the synthesizer is a . . . friend, I could almost say, assisting me in expressing myself, particularly on *Evil*."

Evil, the final track on "Music Of My Mind", is a moving ballad in which Steve laments the terrible powers that have been unleashed by human cruelty. His voice is accompanied on the track by an eerie synthesizer part, adding an extra dimension to the song's impact. Elsewhere on the album, synthesizers and other electronic instruments and recording techniques are used to create a totally new sound for Stevie. One device in particular that he depended on a lot for this album was the voice "bag", which he'd heard on the "Head Band" album. The bag, a synthesizer sound triggered by the player's mouth, offered a widely expanded range for Stevie's vocals.

Love Having You Around, the opening track on "Music Of My Mind", demonstrates the novelty of Steve's conception. Dense layers of thickly recorded electric piano and processed clavinet parts urge the song on in some cosmic

When Stevie's contract expired in May 1971, he spent almost a year in the studio experimenting in ways Motown had never previously enabled him to do.

taffy pull of toe-tapping funk. If *Do Yourself A Favor* was a marked departure from Stevie's previous recordings, this sound is light years ahead of what he had been doing at Motown.

The key to Stevie's new sound was that he no longer had to use Motown's studios to record. The Motown sound that had revolutionized hit singles earlier in the sixties was woefully inadequate for the technological advances in recording available from the start of the seventies. With the help of his new engineers, Stevie got sounds he'd never dreamed of before.

Love Having You Around uses treated vocal overdubs and the distorted "bag" voice sound for a wide variety of effects which Stevie put to good advantage in his highly inventive rhythm arrangement. A bleating trombone solo from Art Baron fills out the track's unusual character.

Keep On Running, the LP's most exciting cut, takes the same ideas another step further, driving the multi-layers of sound into a frenzied dervish dance of intensity. *Sweet Little Girl* also relies on a similar approach, breaking from a shuffling, bluesy harmonica statement to rocking, percussive keyboards layers. The song finished with a slow, Isaac Hayes-style rap section with Stevie's grunting, sexy vocals filtered for maximum impact.

"Music Of My Mind" contains several excellent love songs that continue what was clearly Stevie's strong point at Motown. Both *I Love Every Little Thing About You* and *Happier Than The Morning Sun* are simple and beautiful love songs that rely only incidentally on the augmented electronic sound. Written in the same fashion as previous successes such as *My Cherie Amour* and *Never Dreamed You'd Leave In Summer*, the songs show Stevie still developing as a songwriter. *Happier Than The Morning Sun* relied on production techniques similar to those on the Beatles' "Abbey Road" LP.

Superwoman, a song written about the problems Stevie was having in his relationship with Syreeta, anticipated the break-up of their marriage not long after the album was released. The album is marked by the unity of Steve's conception in playing all of the instruments and singing most of the vocals, with the exception of a guitar solo by Buzz Feiten on *Superwoman*, and Art Baron's trombone solo.

Stevie's touch is so deft he makes the performances, which were meticulously overdubbed over a long period of time, seem spontaneous. He can mimic his instruments with his singing and vice versa, subtly and with great emotional precision, as on the light touch of *Happier Than The Morning Sun*, or off-handedly in powerful surges, on blasting tracks like *Keep On Running*.

"When I recorded 'Music Of My Mind'," he explains, "I didn't have a band then, I didn't have anybody. I just had myself. I wanted to learn to do this. Plus the time involved, it had taken me longer to explain what I was talking about than I really wanted to take. It wasn't bad though, because this is something I really wanted to do. I was very happy with the way it turned out. I wanted to express the way I would have everything sound, the way I would do everything, so I played all the instruments to get that. And basically too because I was using the synthesizer, which is a totally different, whole new world altogether."

Margouleff and Cecil were invaluable in teaching Stevie the use of the synthesizer. At around the time the album was released Stevie gave an explanation of the instrument: "A synthesizer has to be programmed. It consists of seven or eight oscillators and the sound has to be created, because it's just another electrical impulse. With it you have the ability to shape the melody into any form you desire, attack, sustain, decay, release, or the combination of those can be done any way you want, to create the sound. You can use more than one oscillator. You can put two tones together which makes the note sound fatter. You can have them tuned in fifths, or whatever is appropriate for the song you're gonna do.

"You can only play one note at a time with the synthesizer. They do have some polyphonic boards that are maybe able to play two or three to four notes at the same time, but that's in a relatively early stage. They're not really perfected yet. So I use the Moog for certain horn lines, but it really is not so much as to imitate a particular instrument as to make the horizon for an instrument even wider. I'm not a synthesist completely myself."

After having asked for his release from Motown and using his earnings to record the kind of material Motown would never let him do, it might seem strange that, after shopping around the industry for a deal, Stevie eventually went back to that company and signed a new contract. "Observing where I was at," he concludes, "I decided that I wanted to remain a part of what I was already involved with."

Stevie had wrestled with the idea of the Motown "family" and what, if any, relation he had with it: "It could have been because I was loyal to some of the people there, but as for 'The Motown Family', it's very difficult to keep a relationship like that when things are moving and people are living in all different parts of the world."

The remark about different parts of the world refers to Motown's corporate move to Los Angeles, which took effect around the same time that Stevie moved to New York. Stevie felt that Motown was his home in a way, but at the same time he realized that the company was changing, and if the changes were to be beneficial to him, he would have to force Motown's hand: "I knew that I couldn't forever jump up and down and do *Fingertips*. I basically wanted to stay with

Motown. I've been with them since the beginning, and I felt that I would like to be one of the pioneers of seeing it change, get into a new direction. I knew the company, and I knew the people, and all I had to do was somehow convince Gordy, and part of my convincing had been done when I split. I knew that a lot of the emotions that existed were because of the fact that I was young, as opposed to looking at me as being a *man*. They were looking at the past, when I was Little Stevie Wonder running up and down the street. So they had another kind of attachment, and it was sort of an insult or hurt to them when I did split, because they could only relate back to the beginning."

The contract Johannen Vigoda negotiated for Stevie with Motown gave him unprecedented creative freedom with the company and allowed him to maintain control of his publishing while getting a very favorable percentage of the moneys earned from the sale of his records. The

instrument for Stevie to control the copyright on his songwriting was Black Bull Publishing Company. At the same time he formed his own production company, Taurus Productions. Motown had been able to cut an unreasonable deal with the under-age Stevie – after a decade of hit singles and several successful albums, the idea that Motown only owed him one million dollars bordered on insult. From 1972 on, when "Music Of My Mind" was released, Stevie would finally get a fair share of the money his records made.

"It was a very important contract for Motown," says Vigoda, "and a very important contract for Stevie, representing the artists of Motown. He broke tradition with the deal, legally, professionally – in terms of how he could cut his records and where he could cut – and in breaking tradition he opened up the future for Motown. That's what they understood. They never had an *artist* in thirteen years. They had single records, they managed to create a name in certain areas, but they never came through with a major, major artist."

Stevie had Motown over a barrel, but it was the only way to salvage the association. "They were upset at first," he says. "But they began to understand – later. Whatever peak I had reached doing that kind of music, I had reached. It was important for them to understand we were going nowhere."

Stevie's aim was to make album-length statements not limited by the restrictions of having to come up with hit singles. "They weren't into albums much because they didn't have the market for it, they didn't deal with an album-buying audience. The only hassle with them was the lack of understanding, you know. But after I made my agreement with them again and we came to an understanding of what was gonna happen, it was cool." Fortunately for Stevie, "Music Of My Mind" did yield one commercial hit, *Superwoman*, which Motown released as a double A-side.

Under the conditions of the contract, Motown was in effect forced to accept whatever Steve delivered to them. (The "Greatest Hits Vol. II" LP they released during 1971 while Stevie was recording "Music Of My Mind" was the last product Motown put out under the terms of the old contract.) When Stevie submitted the dense, experimental "Music Of My Mind", it didn't

Left and right: Stevie never stopped performing, pouring out innovative ideas, and melodies of increasing complexity.

please the Motown executives, who listened in vain for the hit singles that were their bread and butter. Under the old contract Stevie would never have been permitted to release a record like that, but though it was not a blockbuster album commercially, "Music Of My Mind" alerted music fans around the world that Stevie Wonder was embarking on a new career. The ground swell of interest created by the album paved the way for Stevie's future success, and helped expand Motown into a competitive framework for the seventies.

Stevie Wonder had taken a bold step and stubbornly pulled it off. Ira Tucker, who would become Stevie's publicist and aide-de-camp, summed up the audacity of the move: "He had enough insight to see what he needed to sustain Stevie Wonder as an individual, not just as a product of a record company. It's kind of awesome. I tend to think he had it all figured out from the time he was fourteen."

10. Talking Book

"Music Of My Mind" proved that Stevie Wonder was not limited to the narrow definition of black performers allowed by Motown's approach. "Categorization can be the death of an artist. It's his whole thing – the concept of a black artist. All that 'Oh Stevie – he's a soul man.' That kind of thing. It can kill an artist."

Critical reaction to "Music Of My Mind" proved Stevie's instincts were right. "One man recordings have been tried by performers as diverse as Paul McCartney and Sidney Bechet," wrote Don Heckman in the *New York Times*, "but no one has brought off the complicated trick of playing most – or all – of the parts better than Wonder has in this collection." Listeners were impressed and delighted by the warm, human touch Stevie was able to bring to the synthesizer. "It's almost tactile the way he forces those electronic circuits to emit soulful, moving, tremendously delicate melodies," explained *Melody Maker*. "Wonder's main contribution is that he's made the synthesizer a living instrument." It's interesting to reflect on how few musicians over a decade later have managed to make synthesizers sound like anything more than glorified rhythm machines.

After Stevie proved he could record a different kind of music than people expected of him, he still had to do something about translating his new music to a concert setting. Motown had never prepared him for this – their approach was to package acts interchangeably, dress them up in suits, put together a big band accompaniment with arranger and run through the Vegas-style lounge act. While Stevie was making the ground-breaking statement "Music Of My Mind" he wasn't playing the showcase clubs and theaters where serious rock 'n' roll was being presented, he was doing five shows a day in an Apollo revue and playing midnight sets after the movies were over at the Brooklyn Fox.

This wasn't merely bad judgment on Motown's part. The company ran a tight ship and it was not in Motown's best interests to let their artists have too much independence. Even though Stevie had signed a new contract that dealt favorably with royalties and creative control, Motown could pretty much support and promote the product as they wished.

Fortunately the new relationship with Motown permitted Stevie to look for help elsewhere if he needed it. He asked the New York-based public relations firm Wartoke Concern to help him with promotion. Wartoke had an excellent reputation in the music field after handling media coverage of the Woodstock Festival, and its three partners – Pat Costello, Rod Jacobson and Jane Friedman – were able to give Steve the personal attention he needed.

While Stevie began to put together his band, Wonderlove, based around guitarist Buzz Feiten, bassist Scott Edwards and drummer Greg Copeland, Wartoke began promoting him in areas that had never previously covered Stevie Wonder. "I put him on *What's My Line* and *I've Got A Secret* – TV shows he'd never appeared on before," says Jane Friedman. "Anybody could have done it, it was a matter of picking up the phone and saying 'Would you like to have Stevie Wonder on the show?' and they'd say 'Of course.' We were good for him because we had the idea that what he needed was to expand his audience. We were able to identify the need."

Without management or personal direction from the connections that had run his life until he came of age, Stevie was heavily influenced by the underground music scene in New York and cultivated a closer relationship with the rock audience. He began to do more interviews in the rock press, and was introduced by Wartoke to more rock musicians. In a masterful stroke, Wartoke arranged to have Stevie open for the Rolling Stones on their up-coming summer 1972 North American tour.

"We took some of the Faces down to the Brooklyn Fox to see Stevie," recalls Jane Friedman. "They were big fans and were really excited to meet him. At the time Stevie was a legend but he just wasn't happening. We knew he could sell a million albums, but he had no white audience for concerts because he was never accessible to the white audience. The first thing we did was put him on the Stones tour. Pat Costello was close friends with Sharon Lawrence and Sharon Lawrence was working with the Stones – she thought it was a good idea, and she helped convince the Stones it would be a good idea to take Stevie on the road."

It was a bit of an ironic turnabout for Stevie to open the Rolling Stones tour – in 1964 the Stones had opened U.S. shows for Little Stevie Wonder.

The excitement of preparing for the Rolling Stones tour took some of the sting out of Stevie's break-up with his Syreeta. Steve's explanation of the split suggested that their personalities had clashed strongly. "She's a Leo, and I'm a Taurus," he's often said of their break-up. "They're two fixed signs, and I'm awful stubborn."

One of the songs from "Music Of My Mind", *Superwoman*, may have been influenced by the troubles between the couple. The song is a complaint about a woman who tries to "boss the bull around". With Stevie and Syreeta both pursuing their careers, and Stevie spending virtually all his time in the studio, it's easy enough to understand how there might have been friction.

Syreeta may also have balked at some of Stevie's more conservative views on marriage. "A woman's supposed to take care of a man domestically and spiritually. And the man has to make sure there's something in the home to cook. If the woman keeps the character of herself, that's cool."

"A black man is not complete without a woman," he told the *Afro-American* newspaper. "He needs a woman, not as a crutch or a substitute for his mother, but as a *woman*. She should be intelligent, warm, black-oriented and cookin' at both ends."

Despite their divorce, Steve and Syreeta remained close and Stevie worked with her musically, producing her first two albums. "We have a very beautiful relationship," he insists, "that's still a beautiful love for each other. It's like a love and respect for each other that will forever exist. I think that because you can't make it in your intimate things, or being married to each other, then I think it should just be stricken. Because

what happens I think is that sometimes you can get so *possessive*; and that a woman can need certain things that if she doesn't always have it becomes a drag. And then a dude needs a certain kind of freedom – especially *me*.

"I just wasn't really ready to get married," he concludes. "I think the beauty of going together and being close is so beautiful that sometimes when you get married you feel that you blow it. You get into some other kind of things. You know, it depends on whether the minds are in unison. You have to communicate. And I wasn't really communicating; to a certain extent I was, but then again I wasn't. There were hassles and other things that involved me finding myself."

Whatever the differences were between Steve and Syreeta, their marriage did not end in bitterness, but understanding. "I feel the same way that Stevie does," was Syreeta's succinct summing up. "We both haven't lost anything, but gained a friend for a lifetime." It's interesting to note that Stevie showed himself to be a bit more upset by the break-up. A close friend said of him around the time: "Syreeta had left him and it was a big pain in his heart."

The warm-up spot at a Rolling Stones concert is a difficult position to fill. Hostile crowds impatient to see the Stones have heckled some top groups off the stage over the years, but Stevie came as close to upstaging the Stones as possible with an astonishing set.

Stevie describes his involvement with the Stones tour in an off-handed way. "A friend of a friend of a friend of somebody at Wartoke got in touch with somebody at William Morris and said they wanted me to do this tour. So from there we just met, got together for rehearsals, then started touring. Wonderlove, my band, was with me. I had some things already scheduled before the tour that I had to make, so we ended up rehearsing one day, but everything went real smooth. The set we did didn't involve as much detail as our usual sets do."

Despite the obvious promotional value the tour offered, working with the Rolling Stones had its drawbacks. Steve later maintained that parts of the agreement were not fulfilled: "I think if people see you coming on, it doesn't matter where you are in the show. I enjoyed *the people* involved. We didn't get much coverage from a lot of the press and a lot of the radio stations and stuff, a lot of times the promoter didn't have our

names up on the billboard, and they did promise us they would.

"If I had it to do over again, I'd insist on certain things being handled differently. It's not so important for me, or my ego, as it is for my fans, who come to the concerts because I am appearing on them. And there are other things I'd like to see handled differently: the amount of time I have to play, and the way the publicity is handled."

Jeffi Powell, one of the publicists at Wartoke, noted that Stevie was discriminated against by the national press. "I called every paper in every city along the tour," she recalls, "and kept getting the same answer over and over. They simply refused to cover a black act. It was the same way with the radio stations — even when he had a hot album out, the stations refused to play Stevie because he was a black act. Stevie had a lot to do with breaking the color line at that time in rock 'n' roll."

Stevie's lack of management coupled with Motown's apparent unwillingness to help him out compounded his problems. "On the Rolling Stones tour Motown did nothing to promote

Stevie or to insure that he was taken care of properly," points out Jane Friedman. "He had no manager, and somebody has to see to these sort of things. On most of the dates Stevie Wonder's name never appeared on the marquee. We used to fight with promoters every day to try to get his name on the marquee and make sure it was spelled right. Motown did nothing to promote 'Music Of My Mind' during that tour, either."

For Stevie, the worst moment on the tour came when his drummer, Greg Copeland, suddenly left the band without warning. "My drummer had a nervous breakdown. The gig was in Fort Worth and I told him he rushed the tempo and the tempo was messed up, and he said 'I didn't rush it too much', and I said 'Yes you did.' He said 'I'll tell you what. *You* play the Goddamn drums,' and he split. He left right there. It was the excitement of the tour. The excitement, the pressures, and I think his wife wanted to be home too . . . So the drummer told me to play the drums. He said '*You* play the drums, you're a drummer, you play the drums and sing at the same time and play your harmonica too!' He was very upset.

Stevie at the drums in 1972. The release from his contract on his twenty-first birthday gave him the freedom to play where and with whom he liked.

now, even though I don't profess to know exactly what's going to happen in the future. I don't think *1984* frightened me as much as it made me think."

Big Brother gave an indication of the kind of commitment Steve was prepared to give to promoting his beliefs: "If I can do anything to help my people in respect of black pride, help the black people, then I'll do it. Because I think black people in America have had the most unfortunate changes put on them of any black people in the world."

Despite the fact that U.S. President Richard M. Nixon had personally received Stevie in the Rose Garden of the White House to present him with an award, Stevie maintained an aggressive stance against policies he considered to be unfair. Even though he didn't use drugs himself, Stevie appeared with John Lennon at a Detroit benefit for White Panther Party leader John Sinclair, who'd been jailed on a ten-year sentence for possession of two marijuana cigarettes.

On 24 May, 1973, Stevie attended the funeral of Cloephus Glover, a black child who was killed by a New York City detective. After singing a soft eulogy as the funeral procession left the church, Steve told reporters, "I have followed the case. It brings America down another notch in my book. I hope that black people realize how serious things are and do something serious about it."

The event had such a marked effect on Steve that he often brought the incident up during the following year. "Black people are just now beginning to find their identity, and that's good," he told the Minneapolis *Twin Cities Courier*. "It's unfortunate that tragic things have to bring us together, such as the ten year old boy that was killed by a policeman in New York a few weeks ago. That brought hundreds of people to the funeral, including myself, but after everybody leaves only the mother will feel the pain."

At other times Steve tried to encourage black people to do something about their problems in his public appearances. "Black people have a serious problem because we are not united," he told the Baltimore *Afro-American*. "Everybody else is together. We must learn to appreciate ourselves. We have to learn to appreciate the accomplishments of our forefathers, like Nat Turner, Frederick Douglass and George Washington Carver.

"But it seems that so many people just don't understand. I hate to sound pessimistic, but it will take people many years to realize the true meaning of Malcolm X's message. I may sound pessimistic, but we have serious problems that have to be dealt with. That man in [Washington] D.C. [Nixon] is cutting off all these programs and holding back funds. Who do you think it's hurting? The black man . . . we have always been the last to get and the first to have it taken away."

Stevie's commitment to social improvement wasn't limited to any single cause. He participated in a number of benefits for the blind, and appeared at Philharmonic Hall in New York with Ray Charles and Al Hibbler for the "Out of Sight Night" in May, 1973. "People have so many distorted ideas about blind people and their supposedly 'limited' range of activities," Stevie said. "Many people seriously believe that my daily schedule, for example, consists of listening to my music and just sitting around or sleeping when no one is leading me around by the hand. Man, if they knew how aware and concerned and involved in life blind people are. In many instances, more so than their sighted brothers. To my way of thinking, there are many ways of being handicapped, and they certainly aren't all physical. And the really biggest handicap I see around me every day is in people who lack a sense of communication."

In some ways, Stevie's fame did keep him from developing certain skills blind people learn. He had been constantly surrounded with aides since childhood, so he rarely had to get around on his own. But he never let his lack of sight hold him back from pursuing activities not usually associated with the blind. He goes to a lot of movies, picking up the action from the soundtrack even though he can't see the screen. He also prides himself in his physical abilities: "I really love to bowl. I'm fantastic. But I blow it when I'm happy-footed. There's a special lane, with a guiding rod, for the blind."

Steve uses his ribald sense of humor to offset part of the social problem created by his blindness. People around him never have to worry about insulting Stevie or hurting his feelings because he constantly jokes about blind people, making fun of the consequences of his own inability to see and ridiculing others for different kinds of blindness. One of the favorite phrases he uses to describe someone disapprovingly is to say: "He's too preoccupied with his blindness."

11. Visions

Less than two years after taking control of his own musical direction, Stevie Wonder had it made. During a spectacular performance at New York's Carnegie Hall the show was stopped and Ewart Abner led a procession of Motown executives on stage for an elaborate presentation ceremony. Stevie was given a gold album representing one million dollars in sales for the "Talking Book", and a platinum single representing two million single records sold of *Superstition*.

Stevie went on to garner rave reviews for both himself and Wonderlove at concerts across the country. *Superstition* had hit the Number One position on the U.S. charts, the first time Stevie had earned that slot since *Fingertips Part II*, and *You Are The Sunshine Of My Life* was about to give him back-to-back Number Ones in the U.S. for the first time in his career.

His lifestyle had gone through extraordinary changes. Whereas a few years before he was limited to a tiny allowance and had to con tape recorders out of Motown in order to work on song ideas at home, now he had as much money as he wanted. Stevie poured his money back into music, buying instruments, studio time and the most elaborate tape recorders he could get his hands on.

One aspect of his lifestyle that did not change was his penchant for going without sleep. Making music was such an obsession with him that he kept a clavinet and an expensive tape recorder within arm's reach at all times, even when he was on the road, so he could immediately put down an idea at any time of the day or night. His personal valet at the time, Charlie Collins, related: "Sometimes he'll call me at two in the morning and he'll say 'Charlie, come to the room right away!' I ask him is there anything wrong, and he tells me, 'No, but I just got this song and you've got to hear it.' He's just waked up, you know, and a tune is in his head. It doesn't come from a dream necessarily; he just wakes up and it's there."

Stevie was absorbing musical influences wherever he could find them. In early 1973 he became avidly interested in reggae and talked about it enthusiastically with anyone who would listen. "There's a lot of great ethnic Jamaican music," he pointed out at the time, "and there's many people going over to record to get the right sound — some of it I really like, such as Johnny Nash."

The conditions of his revised contract with Motown gave Stevie the opportunity to produce records, and now that he had demonstrated his commercial instincts, Motown was more than happy to hook him up with their most important groups. The Supremes had been having trouble coming up with hits since lead singer Diana Ross left the group, and Motown arranged for Stevie to produce them. He had a strong idea about how to approach the project, a song called *Bad Weather*. "Jean Terrell has been singing a little bit too pretty, maybe to try to fill in for Diana — but there is only one Diana. And what we've tried to do is get more funk into the sound."

Stevie also produced Syreeta's second album in 1973, maintaining a healthy working relationship with her despite their divorce. The record, which would be released in 1974, was called "Stevie Wonder Presents Syreeta" even though it was the second LP he produced for her. As he did with "Syreeta", Stevie used Wonderlove as the session band: guitarists Mike Sembello and Marlo Henderson; bassist Reggie McBride; drummer Ollie Brown; trumpeter Steve Madaio; tenor saxophonist Dennis Mourouse. As usual a superb chorus of vocalists worked the backing vocals: Minnie Riperton, Deniece Williams, Lani Groves, Shirley Brewer and Anita Sherman. Stevie wrote five songs for the project, including the classic *Cause We've Ended Now As Lovers*, (which Jeff Beck cut on "Blow By Blow") and co-wrote the other five with Syreeta.

Most of Steve's energy was directed toward his next album, which went through a variety of changes while it was being put together. For a

while Steve referred to the upcoming LP as "The Easter Album". "It's the last days of life, of beauty," he said. "All the horrors and hypocrisy in the world today. People neglecting other people's problems. It's what needs doing, socially, spiritually and domestically. I can only do it through song, and I try to be positive about it."

Death and destruction were odd topics for someone to be concentrating on at the peak of his career, but Stevie always had a deeply melancholic side, and he took the American political situation following Nixon's landslide 1972 Presidential election victory very hard.

He wrote an extraordinary number of songs for the album that would eventually be released under the title "Innervisions". It is estimated that by the time "Innervisions" was released, Stevie had between 400 and 1,000 unreleased songs stockpiled. Robert Margouleff and Malcolm Cecil had the unenviable task of cataloging this backlog of material, which they recorded alphabetically by song title in a volume they referred to as the "Blue Book".

During this period, Stevie slept on average only about four hours a night, and would work at stretches of 48 hours without a break. The intensity of his commitment was underscored by the fact that "Innervisions" was the first album written entirely by himself, without the aid of an outside lyricist.

"Innervisions" turned out to be a catalog of Stevie's current concerns, particularly the issues that were bothering him. The album opener *Too High*, sets a chilling tone for the proceedings, with a macabre tale meant to illustrate the dangers of drug use. The opening passage uses shuffling drums, a rhythmic synthesizer figure and vocalists phrasing a unison melodic statement with electric piano to evoke a hypnotic mood, which Steve breaks with his vocal in clipped accents with a phased treatment to the sound that creates a hallucinogenic effect. The song describes drug experiences accurately for a professed non-user, but by the end of the tune the protagonist has died.

Visions, which Stevie has often pointed out as one of his favorite songs, flows out of a beautiful instrumental mood created by Malcolm Cecil on bass, Dean Parks on acoustic guitar and David T. Walker on guitar. The song paints scenarios of the kind of world Stevie would like to see, where people love each other, have enough to eat and

hate is non-existent. Nevertheless there's a world-weariness in the chorus, when Stevie realizes his vision of a perfect world is only a daydream.

"Innervisions" is suffused with a sense of impending doom that goes beyond Stevie's warnings about the state of the world — it's almost as if he sensed the impending tragedy that would nearly take his life later in the year. *Jesus Children Of America* is a compelling mixture of these themes — Stevie contemplates the passion of Christ dying on the cross in several contexts. On one hand he sees the "holy rollers" who use religious evangelism for their own personal political and financial gains; on the other hand he sees the simplicity and love of young children as the hope for the future. He adds his own spiritual point in the last verse, endorsing transcendental meditation for the peace of mind it offers. Similarly, *Higher Ground* is charged with a sense of desperation, of time running out. In the song Stevie alludes to former lives and thanks God for letting him keep trying to reach a more elevated spiritual plane.

The album's most memorable song, *Living For The City*, became its most pervasive track (*Higher Ground,* making No. 1, was the biggest hit). Steve's political sensibility is at its keenest here as he tells the story of a poor southern black who arrives in New York City by bus, gets framed and thrown unjustly in jail by the song's end.

"I think the deepest I really got into how I feel about the way things are was in *Living For The City*," says Stevie. "I was able to show the hurt and the anger, you know. You still have that same mother that 'scrubs the floors for many', she's still doing it. Now what is that about. And that father who 'works some days for fourteen hours.' I mean it's still happening."

Amazingly, Stevie manages to draw a picture of this dead-end, oppression-ridden lifestyle without sounding bitter or cynical, even managing to leaven the impact with his inimitable sense of humor. In the bridge at the middle of the tune it's hard not to laugh when you hear Stevie's brother, Calvin Hardaway, utter the lines: "New York City, just like I pictured it/ Skyscrapers and everything."

The music of *Living For The City* arose from his own sound-orientated perception of city life. To explain his inspiration at the press preview

Stevie receives a gold disc for the million-selling album "Talking Book".

12. New Life

Steve's recovery from the accident was relatively speedy, considering the severity of the injury, but it was still a slow, painstaking process for him. Painful recurring headaches forced him to cancel a planned press conference at first. When a rescheduled meeting with the press in mid-September was arranged, Stevie announced: "I feel OK. But I'll have to be on medication for at least another six months. The loss of my sense of taste and smell may be permanent. It goes, then comes back, goes again, comes back. The doctor said I would sometimes get tired, maybe late at night, but I can do it."

Before the accident, Stevie had been at the crest of his popularity, with "Innervisions" posed to pick up where the phenomenal success of "Talking Book" left off. If anything, the accident boosted his popularity. News reports of his condition would be followed on the radio with *Higher Ground*, which became a kind of rallying cry for his recovery. When Stevie returned to the public eye only a few weeks after the near-fatal injury, his fans treated it as a miraculous return from the dead. On 25 September, Stevie appeared on stage during an Elton John concert. "A friend of mine is here," John announced to the sell-out crowd at Boston Gardens. "He was badly hurt in an accident some time ago." That was all the introduction Wonder needed, as he and Elton John waited through an ecstatic fifteen-minute long ovation before playing a medley of *Honky Tonk Women* and *Superstition*.

Full-length concerts, or any kind of touring, were ruled out for the rest of the year, leaving Stevie with more free time than he'd enjoyed in years. Much of it was spent writing songs and working in the studio on his next album, but at the same time he was cultivating an altogether new lifestyle for himself. It was during this period of convalescence that Stevie met Yolanda Simmons, who would later become the mother of his children.

Stevie met Yolanda because of his penchant for answering the phones himself at his publishing company, Black Bull. She had called looking for a secretarial position and got more than she bargained for. "We met on the phone," says Stevie. "I liked the way she sounded, and we became friends. Then it turned into other feelings, which made our friendship more beautiful."

One of Stevie's biggest concerns after his accident was to have children. "When I have children," he said dramatically, "when I express what I have to say, then my life will be over. I always wanted to be a father, but I knew I had to wait till I met the right woman who would give my child the love it needs."

Steve and Yolanda announced their engagement at one point, but never actually got married — the experience of his first marriage, and his own family history, was enough to convince him that there were no guaranteed contracts on love. "We didn't have to do a 'marry me' and 'I marry you' thing," he says of his relationship with Yolanda. "Love is free — it's not about possession."

Another major change in Stevie's post-accident lifestyle was that he became much calmer than anyone remembered him being before — the restless energy was replaced by an inner peace. "I've seen this dude go through a lot of changes," says Ira Tucker, "and I've learned a lot from him. The accident has changed him more than anything; it's really cooled him out. There was a time when if he wasn't playing the piano or singing or listening to tapes, he'd get restless and have to go out and do something, buy this or that, or go to the studio. He never used to sleep. He'd call me at four in the morning and say 'Hey, we gotta go to the studio, right now.' But I think he's over the hump now; he's got an idea of what it's all about. He called me the other morning and he said 'Tuck, when I was out cold in the hospital, did I do a lot of heavy breathing?' I said 'yeah, man, you sure did'. He just said 'I thought so,' and hung up."

It wasn't until the following January that Stevie returned to the concert scene, playing a

twenty-minute set with a four-piece band at the MIDEM convention, the annual international music business meeting, in Cannes, France, followed by four full-length shows with his regular band at London's Rainbow Theatre.

Melody Maker brought the good news back from Cannes. "A taste of real music came on Sunday when Stevie Wonder shone at the opening MIDEM gala," the report went. "It was Stevie Wonder's first concert since his car accident last summer — and he played like he'd never been away. After two hours or so of bland Euro-pop, Wonder provided a small breath of sanity.... Wonder, dressed in Sheik-Afro gown, pounded on the electric piano against a compulsive backdrop created by the band Wonderlove...."

From there he returned to the States in March for a triumphant reunion with his American fans at Madison Square Garden in New York. The show was a marathon performance, covering every phase of Wonder's history, and featured *Contusion*, a brand new instrumental number which started the night off. Shortly into the show flautist Bobbi Humphrey came on stage to jam. Bobbi was in her ninth month of pregnancy, and Stevie asked the crowd to consider how this child would be "Living for the city". He played an outstanding version of the song with the

entire audience chanting an extended, ten minute chorus: "I'm tired, tired of living for the city." The real treat though, was saved until the end, when Roberta Flack, Eddie Kendricks and Sly Stone joined Stevie. The climax of the show came during a bang-up run-through of *Superstition*, which ended up with Sly getting so carried away as the audience chanted his anthem, "higher . . . higher" that he seemed to forget who the glory of the moment belonged to. Steve led him from the stage, gently, but forcefully.

Wonder's band had become an incredibly powerful unit by this time. Though Stevie has always had first-rate guitar players working with him, Michael Sembello, who joined around the time of "Innervisions", was something special. A gifted, creative player schooled in the classics and jazz, he brought a fresh, musicianly sensibility to Steve's band that fitted the advanced ideas Stevie was trying out at the time. Sembello went on to enjoy success as a solo act, scoring a hit single with *Maniac*, a song on the *Flashdance* soundtrack, but his stint with Stevie resulted in a lot of memorable music.

Sembello might have seemed an unlikely choice for Wonderlove. "I was very turned off to commercial music when I started," explains Sembello. "Everybody thinks, 'Well, you played with Stevie Wonder', but I didn't listen to Motown until I was 20. I didn't listen to R&B, I listened to Pat Martino and John Coltrane and Igor Stravinsky. So when I got the gig with Stevie Wonder I was completely unaware of his music."

In fact, Sembello was completely unaware he was even being considered for a job. "I got hooked up with him through an audition at a time when he was moving in a more musical direction," Sembello recalls. "That was around the time of 'Innervisions' and he was trying to get a different caliber of musician, instead of the typical James Brown R&B guitar player. He heard Philadelphia was the den of guitar players and came there and booked this hotel called the Heritage House and held auditions for two days.

"I probably would not have been there had it not been for a friend of mine who came by my house and woke me up and said, 'Let's go to this jam session.' It was real big to go to jams back then. Half way there he said 'Oh by the way, Stevie Wonder's gonna be at this jam session.' He failed to tell me it was an audition, because he

Previous page: *Stevie was back on stage within months of his automobile accident.* Above left: *Stevie flies into London with Motown aides in January 1974, touring again in spite of the recurrent headaches he suffered as a*

knew I wouldn't have gone since I was into my jazz and I couldn't be bothered. So we get down there and there's a big clipboard with about 200 names on it and there's 200 guitar players warming up in this hotel lobby. I said, 'Let's get out of here, this is crazy, it's an audition and we came to jam.' But he went up when nobody was looking and erased the first five names on the list and put ours on so we got in right away. So whoever the top five guys were, I'm sorry.

"So we got in there and I really didn't want to be there. And all these guys, Stevie Wonder was their idol and they knew every tune he'd ever written and were plugged into everything he ever did. I didn't know who he was – seriously, I did not know any of his tunes. But I happened to be a good musician and I had a good ear. He started playing all this off the wall shit, and obviously all these guys are waiting for *Finger-tips* or *Superstition* and he starts going into all this jazz stuff. It was kind of like a game show for guitar players: if you hang in there you get to stay, but if you screw up you were eliminated. You solo and if you fuck up it's thank you, see you later.

"I lasted there about three or four hours and it came down to me and this other guy, and Stevie started playing all this off the wall bebop and modulating keys and it was no problem for me – it was like playing a wedding and very simple. He started playing a song from his new album that wasn't out yet, and I just copped the changes immediately. He said 'How did you do that?' I told him I had a good ear. He said, 'Did you hear my new album yet?' Then he leaned over to one of his promotion guys and said 'Is the album out yet?' and the guy said no. He wanted to know 'How the hell do you know these tunes?' I said 'I don't know the tunes, I'm just guessing where you're gonna go.' He couldn't believe that and said 'You've got the gig.' and I said 'I didn't come here for no gig – I just came here to jam'."

Of course Sembello took the job. "Three days later I was on my way to New York with my guitar, an old Epiphone Broadway, in a case with no handles and a paper bag with my clothes. All the guys in the band had huge Afros and studded jeans and I come in wearing one of those work shirts they put people in prison with and sneakers with holes and a guitar case held together with duct tape. When I walked into that first

result of the accident. Right: *Stevie Wonder performing at the legendary Rainbow Theatre, Finsbury Park, London in January 1974.*

rehearsal I hadn't met anyone in the band, and Marlo Henderson was the other guitar player at the time. He looked at me and then turned to the other guys and said 'Either this guy is the baddest motherfucker or just some hokey guy from Louisiana.' They didn't know where Steve had found me, but they were used to him being a little off the wall anyway. Of course, music transcends all prejudice and boundaries and within about two hours we all became the best of friends."

Sembello grew to respect Stevie's musical genius and is grateful for the experience. "When I was seventeen years old, I was like a sponge," he says. "And being in that group was a learning experience. He broke down a lot of my musical prejudices and you can't help but be influenced when you're that young. I look at it as a very rare opportunity — like going to a school that hardly anyone gets a chance to go to. With my background it was a strange kind of mutation, this Stravinsky and Martino buff hooking up with R&B music. I feel Stevie educated us all, and he

taught me the missing link that I didn't have at that time which was feel and feeling, learning to play from the heart, sing from the heart. I had all the technical ability in the world and could play like the fastest guitar player in the West, but he was the one who taught me the most about feel."

At the Grammy awards for achievement in the American record industry in March, 1974 Wonder was presented with an incredible five prizes — best R&B vocal performance and best songwriter prizes for *Superstition*; best pop vocal performance for *You Are The Sunshine Of My Life*; best album of the year and best engineered recording awards for "Innervisions".

Stevie continued to produce other artists as well. He went back into the studio with Syreeta to polish up the tapes for "Stevie Wonder Presents Syreeta". "We were held up by Stevie's accident," Syreeta explained at the time in a *Disc* interview, "and then when we'd completed it, we decided that it was a bit too melancholy as it stood, so we altered a few tracks to make it sound slightly more cheerful ... Our divorce

Above left: *Stevie jamming with Johnny Winter and Dr. John at the Bottom Line nightclub in February 1974.* Above right: *The finale of Stevie's first solo concert after his accident, held at Madison Square Garden. Stevie was joined*

hasn't caused any problems in our musical relationship. There'll always be that tie between us. There's no reason why we can't continue to work together."

In 1974 Stevie produced and played on Minnie Riperton's "Perfect Angel" LP. Riperton, an incredible vocalist with a five octave range, had long been a favorite of Stevie's. She was shocked to learn that he was a fan of hers when they first met in 1971. "Everybody was trying to meet Stevie," the now-deceased Riperton recalled in a 1974 interview. "It was his first step, he was starting to produce and I was really into his music – so I made it quick. I didn't want to bore him or take up his time, so I said 'I just want to thank you for your beautiful music. You've made me and my family very happy.' As I was leaving he said, 'Oh thank you, sister. What's your name?' When I told him 'Minnie', he freaked. 'You're not Minnie Riperton, are you?' He started jumping around. 'Oh my God! Is this a dream? I must be in heaven. You're an angel. Your music is fantastic. I've gone through three of your

"Come To My Garden" albums, where can I get another? Oh this is so beautiful. Thank *you* for the work *you've* done!' "

Stevie also wrote a song in 1974 for the band called Rufus that made the reputation of lead singer Chaka Khan. The song, *Tell Me Something Good*, was written especially for her. Stevie had heard the band's version of his tune *Maybe Your Baby* on the first Rufus album and showed up unannounced at the studio where the band was recording its second LP with *Tell Me Something Good*. The song would eventually win a Grammy at the 1975 awards. That same year Stevie produced a couple of tracks for the Jackson Five and played harmonica on Dave Mason's "It's Like You Never Left" LP.

His biggest production project, of course, was his own LP, "Fulfillingness First Finale". In assembling the record Wonder was faced with an interesting dilemma – there were literally hundreds of songs left over from sessions for previous albums, some completely recorded. "There's a lot of songs left over from the 'Talking

on stage by Roberta Flack (far left), Sly Stone (center),
Eddie Kendricks, of the Temptations (second from right),
along with his own backing singers from Wonderlove,
Shirley Brewer, Deniece Williams and Lori Groves.

101

Book' and 'Innervisions' sessions which I would like to use", he explained at the time. "I'll have to listen to them and decide. When I feel right I'll make a decision."

As usual, Stevie was writing plenty of new songs as he went along, songs which reflected his new ideas about life. "When you come that close to death, you realize a lot of things about yourself," he says, "You realize how important time is, how it's necessary to make the best use of it. But you also learn it's important to take time out to relax. Like one of the things I did when I came back to LA for the first time since the accident was to go down to the park and just lay on the grass for an hour or so. I might not have done that a year ago. You get so caught up in recording and touring. But it's important to just cool out. It's important for me and for the music. That's where the music comes from."

Just as there had been fears for Steve's health after the accident, then concerns if he could play

again, now that it was time to make a record, people speculated about his ability to continue writing great material. Steve's reaction to such speculation was to push himself to new creative heights and write music that surpassed his previous efforts. He became obsessed with the idea of transcending the "Innervisions/Talking Book" sound and ended up scrapping most of the ideas carried over from those projects as he assembled a record of massive scope. In a dream he saw the title "Fulfillingness First Finale", a name which he felt conveyed the meaning that one stage in life had ended and another was beginning.

"I know everyone was expecting another 'Innervisions,'" Stevie said at the time of the album's release, "and I hate that categorization. People categorize because they can't get used to change.

" 'Innervisions' was a very important album to me. But this, too, is a very important album, a

Above left: *A meeting of the greats: Stevie joins Little Richard (second left), Roberta Flack and Chuck Berry (right) at the 1974 Grammy Awards.*

Above right: *Stevie's style was irresistible and his accident showed no signs of slowing him down.*

very personal one. It was originally supposed to be a double album, but we changed our minds. It wasn't that I tried to make it different from 'Innervisions', it just came out that way. My music reflects what is happening in my life and a lot of things happened between 'Innervisions' and 'Fulfillingness'."

"Fulfillingness' First Finale" is the obvious product of Stevie's augmented self-awareness and spirituality following the accident. Many artists recover from a brush with death to produce an extraordinary work of spiritual understanding – Bob Dylan's post-motorcycle accident "John Wesley Harding" album comes to mind – and "Fulfillingness" is the message Stevie brought back from the underworld, in what is arguably his finest album.

Smile Please is a wonderfully optimistic note on which to open the record, one of the few tracks not stamped with Stevie's one-man band recording sound, as guitarist Michael Sembello, bassist Reggie McBride and percussionist

Bobbye Hall augment Steve's keyboards. Sembello's beautiful intro breaks to Stevie's warm vocal, which urges the listener to relax and enjoy life in a stunning series of images glorifying human happiness. The melody and vocal harmonics combine for an astonishingly blissful effect.

With *Heaven Is 10 Zillion Light Years Away* Steve addresses the existence and nature of a supreme deity, insisting that if God does exist, "we need him now". The idea that heaven is so far removed conceptually from our lives is wrong, Stevie says, asking why they don't say that hate is so far away, and pointing out that God is inside every one of us. All you have to do is "open your heart" and "you can feel his spirit". Stately layers of keyboards, with the Moog bass again playing a prominent part, carry the song into the spectacular chorus when Paul Anka, Syreeta Wright, Shirley Brewer and Larry Latimer join in for the handclapping and testifying sessions. Stevie is at his Baptist preacher best on his overdubbed vocal fills, shouting "sinner" re-

Stevie pickin' chicken at the Bottom Line Club early in 1974. The scar from his head injury can clearly be seen on his forehead.

peatedly back and forth across the stereo image.

Too Shy To Say is an exquisite love song with Sneaky Pete Kleinow playing a steel guitar which sounds as beautiful and other worldly as Stevie's most imaginative synthesizer textures, accompanied by a subtle, understated acoustic bass part from James Jamerson.

Boogie On Reggae Woman breaks the mood with a thumping dance groove powered by more impossible synthesizer rhythmic sequences from Stevie. Wonder's musical imagination is so unique that he could record rhythmically supple material such as this, undisputably dance music, without making it sound like an empty piece of machine-tooled tape loops as many early disco productions sounded.

Minnie Riperton sings backing vocals on Steve's haunting love song *Creepin'*, which has a melodic theme phrased by synthesizers in harmony, reminiscent of *Spooky*, the Classics IV hit from the late sixties.

The album's strongest political message is the sharp-edged, rocking *You Haven't Done Nothin'*, an exhilarating multi-keyboard extravaganza of hissing, pumping percussion sounds punching it out with starship synthesizer riffs, fat mock "horn sections", stabbing clavinet, a meaty bass line supplied by Reggie McBride and inspired vocal group accompaniment from the Jackson Five. The song, which was written with Richard Nixon in mind, was released as a single around the time Nixon was forced to resign from the Presidency in 1974 because of the Watergate scandal.

It Ain't No Use is an interesting love song about the end of an affair, a gorgeous melody embellished by the support vocals of Lani Groves, Minnie Riperton and Deniece Williams. Groves and Williams are joined by Shirley Brewer for the fantastic, jazz-inspired vocal accompaniment on *Bird Of Beauty*, a spectacular companion piece to *Smile Please* that celebrates the joy of being alive. "I meditate but it's a different kind of thing," explains Stevie. "I think, again, observation of your surroundings as well as yourself is the greatest way of having peace within. For instance when I did the song *Bird Of Beauty* I felt God was telling me to take a vacation."

Michael Sembello adds guitar, and a huge chorus made up of Brewer, Williams and the vocal group the Persuasions make *Please Don't Go* one of Stevie's most spirited love songs. Stevie had become increasingly fascinated with Africa around this time, and even talked of moving there. Some fans think that the chanted vocals begging "Please don't go" at the song's end are aimed at Stevie himself. On the fade you can hear him say, "Don't leave Steve".

If *Heaven . . .* articulated the spiritual concerns and *You Haven't Done Nothin'* the moral issues dealt with on the record, *They Won't Go When I Go* combines them in a frighteningly evocative glimpse of hell. The lyrics, for which Stevie relied on Yvonne Wright's assistance (for the only time on the record), work from the premise that Stevie is confident of his own salvation, but "lying friends" and "unclean minds" won't get to the same place. In a brilliant allusion, the song's meaning is amplified by making reference to the Curtis Mayfield line from the pop-gospel classic *People Get Ready* — "There ain't no room for the hopeless sinner."

The synthesizer programming on *They Won't Go When I Go* is particularly effective, contrasting evocatively with a simple classical piano phrase and slowly building emotional intensity in support of the growing dread in the lyric. Wonder singled out Margouleff and Cecil in the album credits for their synthesizer programming on that track.

"The great thing about electronic music," says Stevie, "is you can make things larger than life. You can choose colors, and you can make the sounds of an instrument that does not exist. But I feel you have to stay on the ground, that you can go too far and you lose the people — for me, anyway. You listen to *They Won't Go When I Go*. That'll tell you where I'm going — away from sorrow and hate, up to joy and laughter. I feel *everyone* should be able to grasp what you're doing. It shouldn't be so complicated that it's beyond everyone's capabilities, nor should it be so simple that you cannot use your mind to think about it."

With "Fulfillingness' First Finale" Steve accomplished every detail of his comeback from the accident. Not only had he proven that nothing had been lost by the near-tragedy, he demonstrated that it had helped him arrive at a new level. "The only thing that you can do is be thankful for what you have. You intensify your appreciation for life, become appreciative that you do have a future to look forward to."

13. Contract Time Again

It took Stevie longer to recover completely from the after effects of his auto accident than it appeared because he returned to the public eye so quickly. When he played his Madison Square Garden come-back he was still on medication, and he realized after the show that he wasn't really up to a demanding concert schedule. A planned five week, twenty city tour had to be cancelled.

By September Stevie had recovered his strength sufficiently to embark on "Stevie Wonder's Fall Festival Tour: Wonder Loves You," which played to 35 cities in the U.S. and Japan. In November, Stevie threw a benefit concert at Shaw University, a black college in Raleigh, North Carolina, saving the school from bankruptcy. Los Angeles mayor Tom Bradley declared 1 November "Wonder Day" in Tinseltown.

As 1975 began Steve kept a lower profile, spending most of his time in the studio recording for his next project. He interrupted that work to tour Jamaica, where he came into contact with Bob Marley and the Wailers and thus made his first step into the reggae mainstream that he would come to embrace in a few years. In March, "Fulfillingness' First Finale" won four Grammy awards and Stevie picked up another one for *Living For The City*.

Steve's friendship with Yolanda Simmons had grown into a more meaningful relationship after his divorce from Syreeta. Though Steve was reluctant to re-marry, he and Yolanda decided to begin a family. On Monday, 7 April, 1975, Yolanda gave birth to the couple's first child, a baby girl named Aisha Zakia, African words for "strength and intelligence". The choice of an African name is hardly surprising — since he came of age, Stevie had been interested in exploring his heritage, dropping the hokey suits Motown used to force him to wear on stage in favour of dashikis and flowing robes. He would visit Africa later in 1975.

With Aisha's birth, suddenly Stevie had the responsibilities of a father. Up until this point he lived a freewheeling lifestyle without keeping a fixed address, often staying in hotel rooms close to whatever studio he happened to be working in at the time. Stevie tried to devote more time to family life, purchasing a home in California and a beautiful 100-year-old townhouse on Manhattan's east side. In fact Stevie was to spend much less time at home than he'd anticipated as he became more and more obsessed with his next album project and virtually lived in the recording studio.

What exactly would follow up "Fulfillingness' First Finale" was a burning question to both Motown Records and the rest of the music world. But Stevie hung fire, because the date on which his contract with Motown was due to expire rapidly approached.

Originally "Fulfillingness" was supposed to be a double album, but when it was released as a single LP, Steve assured reporters that the rest of the record would eventually be released as "FFF Part II". "'Fulfillingness' First Finale' was going to be a double album," he said at the time, "but instead we're going to release it in two parts, and I might wait a long time, maybe more than a year after the second record, before I release another album. The title indicates that this is the last of this kind of stuff that I'll be doing — different songs and essentially the same instrumentation. I think my next thing might be a large orchestral thing. A long piece."

Stevie even went as far as playing people tracks from "FFF II", including one in particular called *The Future*, which he says was "fantastically influenced by the SLA [Symbionese Liberation Army] thing. I was watching TV when they had the shoot-out and the fire that burned up all the people and that's when I wrote *The Future*."

"I believe it will clarify a lot of what's on the last album," he said of "FFF II". "It is actually more in-depth."

Meanwhile, though, Steve decided to heat up his contract negotiations with Motown by announcing that he would retire from the music

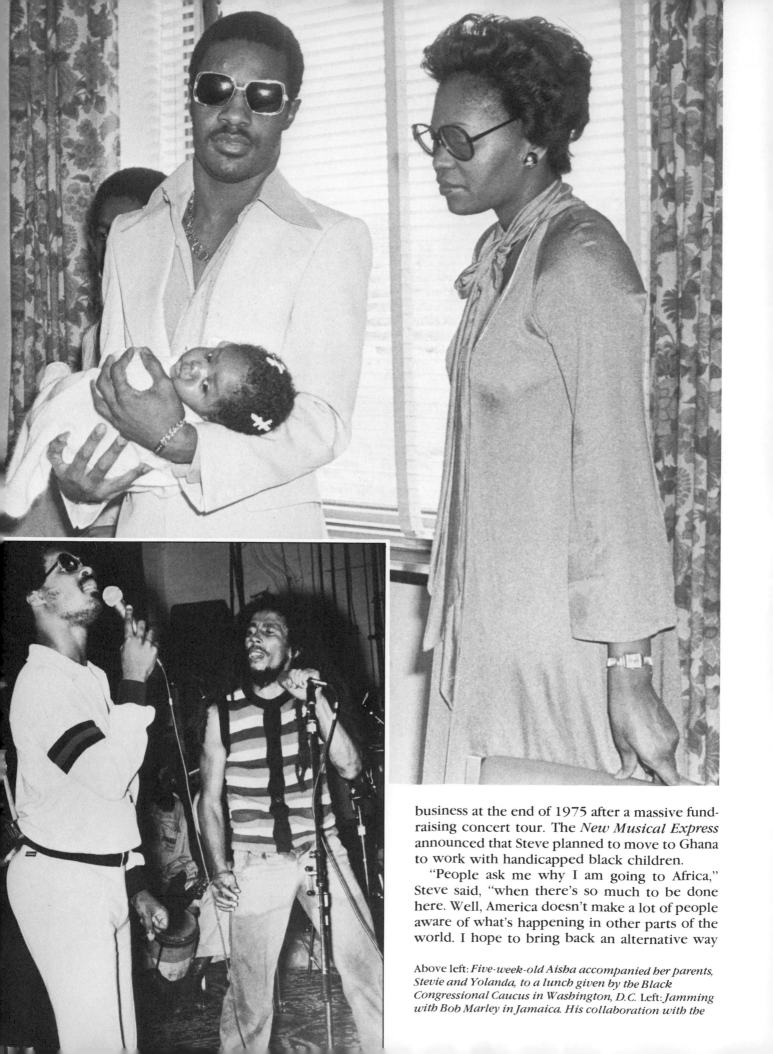

business at the end of 1975 after a massive fund-raising concert tour. The *New Musical Express* announced that Steve planned to move to Ghana to work with handicapped black children.

"People ask me why I am going to Africa," Steve said, "when there's so much to be done here. Well, America doesn't make a lot of people aware of what's happening in other parts of the world. I hope to bring back an alternative way

Above left: *Five-week-old Aisha accompanied her parents, Stevie and Yolanda, to a lunch given by the Black Congressional Caucus in Washington, D.C.* Left: *Jamming with Bob Marley in Jamaica. His collaboration with the*

from Africa. Also I want to do something for blind people over there. Like 40 per cent of the blindness in Ethiopia, for example, is caused by a fly that carries a fungus to the cornea. We have to *do* something about this disease, which is called 'sleeping sickness' and causes blindness. I want to try to set up a foundation to combat this illness.''

While it is probably unfair to doubt the

sincerity of such comments from Stevie, it is also folly to ignore the impact of such a plan on Motown. President Ewart Abner's curt response – "We shall try to point out to Stevie that he can do more good for the cause by raising money in concert than by going out there to work" – indicated that Stevie's statement did have an affect on the company.

Stevie's plans never got very far, and were

acknowledged king of reggae inspired Stevie to produce the extraordinary Masterblaster: Jammin' *in tribute.* Above right: *Celebrating with champagne after another successful show with Yolanda and friends.*

109

soon treated as if they never existed, but the contract negotiations continued to be delicate. Stevie was being actively wooed by a number of other companies, and Motown was well aware that he was not very happy with a lot of the company's business procedures.

Steve himself is extremely generous with his money, contributing lavishly to a large number of charities and taking personal interest in people with severe handicaps and fatal diseases, often making impromptu hospital visits to cheer seriously ill children. In May, 1975 Stevie led "Human Kindness Day", a celebration of humanitarian interests, by playing a free concert to a huge audience on the grassy mall in Washington, D.C. where the great demonstrations of the sixties had taken place. He actively participated in the "One To One" benefits for mentally handicapped children with John Lennon, Sha Na Na and Roberta Flack. You can hear a snatch of them all singing *Give Peace A Chance* on Lennon's "Shaved Fish" album.

In August of 1975 Stevie re-signed with Motown for another seven years, in exchange for guarantees of thirteen million dollars. It was reported to be the largest sum ever advanced to a recording artist at the time. The conditions of the deal gave Steve even more control over his product than the previous contract.

"The future is very positive," Stevie said during celebrations to mark the contract-signing ceremony. "There are faults at Motown, but they can be corrected. If you went somewhere else there'd be other problems — probably a lot

Above: *Lula Hardaway helps her son Stevie cut the cake during his twenty-fifth birthday celebrations. The party was laid on by the organizers of Human Kindness Day, on*

worse ones. I feel comfortable here. I've known some of the people a very long time. They've let me get away with things that other companies may not have allowed."

Though the thirteen million was a significant inducement, Stevie went on to say that he re-signed with Motown because it was a black company. "I'm staying at Motown, because it is the only viable surviving black-owned company in the record industry. Motown represents hopes and opportunity for new as well as established black performers and producers. If it were not for Motown, many of us just wouldn't have had the shot we've had at success and

which Stevie had given a free concert (above left) for 50,000 people at the Washington Monument.

fulfillment. It is vital that people in our business – particularly the black creative community, including artists, writers and producers – make sure that Motown stays emotionally stable, spiritually strong, and economically healthy."

With his long-range future mapped out for seven years, during which time he was required to deliver seven records to Motown, Steve apparently had it made. But for all Steve's good fortune, there were problems. He was well insulated from outsiders by a small army of handlers and hangers-on headed up by his brothers – Milton, who ran his office, and Calvin, who stayed close to Steve's person at all times. Various internal disputes served to create an atmosphere of mistrust and juggling for power in Steve's organization. Perhaps the greatest damage resulting from these problems was the split between Steve and his production team of Robert Margouleff and Malcolm Cecil.

Margouleff and Cecil had nurtured Steve through his first recordings outside Motown's supervision, familiarized him with synthesizer techniques, programmed instruments for him, and provided invaluable critical distance and objective advice on Steve's recordings. They cataloged in meticulous detail song ideas as Steve put them down, kept them handy for future use, and advised him how they could best be developed. The collaboration had produced Steve's finest records – "Music Of My Mind", "Talking Book", "Innervisions" and "Fulfillingness' First Finale". Without them, Steve has failed to this day to match that string of excellence with subsequent releases.

It was clear from remarks made to *Newsweek*'s Maureen Orth in 1974 that Margouleff and Cecil were having trouble with Stevie's people. "The Beatles changed the sixties and Stevie has the power to change the seventies", said Margouleff, "but you have to understand the pressure he's under. Unless he's prepared not to worry so much about his allegiance to the drones, they are going to pull him down and isolate him from the very things that made him good."

Cecil's comments were even more pointed. "Stevie's area of genius is music," he said, "and, in other areas, although he's very competent, he's still only 24. He has to deal with many levels of his reality through the eyes and trust of many other people. I wouldn't put up one minute with the crap his organization puts me through if I didn't believe Stevie has the power to be a very, very important figure, and not just musically. His product does more than sell millions of records. It reaches people and breaks down ethnic barriers. All of a sudden there's money going from the white people to the black people, even if it's only for their bloody music."

Stevie in jocular mood with Billy Preston, Bobbi Humphrey and Yolanda.

Margouleff and Cecil's observations were prophetic — once Steve no longer worked with them, plans for his next album became extremely chaotic. Significantly, Steve had never released double albums while they worked with him, but his next record would be criticized for its longwindedness.

"Songs In The Key Of Life" was produced in absolute chaos. The record was supposedly ready for an entire year before it was finally released in late 1976, just barely in time for eligibility in that year's Grammy awards. At one point a full scale press junket listening party had been arranged, and all the invitations sent, before Steve apparently panicked and pulled the album back to re-mix it further. Motown employees were running around in t-shirts that read "Stevie's Nearly Ready".

When it finally was released, months later, "Songs In The Key Of Life" was hyped as a totally new musical direction for Steve, but in fact it was just a three-record (a free EP was included in the package), overblown rehash of previous ideas, some of them great, but too many merely tedious. *Love's In Need Of Love Today*, the opening track, is pathetic both in recording sound and sentiment compared to his previous work. In the huge booklet that accompanies the record Steve proclaimed to be presenting a philosophy through this music which he called "love mentalism", but the first song fails to start the album off on anything approaching an inspired note. It's fine to say we need less hate and more love, and it's important to say it over and over, but unfortunately, on this record Stevie doesn't back the message with the force of his best music.

Have A Talk With God, written by Steve along with his brother Calvin Hardaway and performed in a rather gimmicky manner by Steve on the synthesizer, sounds positively insincere next to *Heaven Is 10 Zillion Light Years Away* and *They Won't Go When I Go*. From being the powerful force that Steve had previously presented his creator, Steve and Calvin here depict a God who is "the only free psychiatrist".

Village Ghetto Land sets a message about poverty and degradation in a slick and pompous instrumental backing that sounds like nothing so much as the Beatles' *Eleanor Rigby*. Stevie is just too painfully concerned with himself as an *artiste* on this kind of material.

As for *Contusion*, the version recorded here is merely an average fusion track which owes an uncomfortable debt to both Chick Corea's Return To Forever and John McLaughlin's Mahavishnu Orchestra. It is far inferior to the live versions Wonderlove played.

Up to this point nothing on "Key Of Life" sounds like it could have cracked the line-up of any of Stevie's previous four albums. On the other hand, *Sir Duke* ranks with the best material Steve has ever written. The full band definitely helps, as Steve's one-man band sound has apparently run out of ideas on much of this record. Steve comps synthesizer into the outstanding horn chart played by Hank Redd on alto, Raymond Maldonado and Steve Madaio on trumpets and Trevor Lawrence on tenor. The chorus of *Sir Duke* is one of the most inspired moments in Steve's recording history.

The rest of the record runs pretty much to the same form — moments of brilliant clarity in a morass of quicksand. The spectacular *I Wish* uses essentially the same band as *Sir Duke* in a similarly ecstatic rave-up. *Knocks Me Off My Feet* is a beautiful but languid and rambling love song that would have benefited from editing. *Pastime Paradise* combines a rhythm track keyed to Hare Krishna chanters with an uneventful orchestral arrangement and a gospel choir. The idea is fairly interesting first time around, but I doubt if Steve himself still listens to it.

Summer Soft is a nice, unassuming tune distinguished by Ronnie Foster's organ playing and one of Steve's most convincing performances on the record. *Ordinary Pain*, on the other hand, asks for your sympathy in truly unappealing fashion. Steve's capacity for self-pity is as strong as his capacity for moral outrage, and the overkill of his presentation of heartbreak here is merely ineffective. The song is more convincing musically, with Shirley Brewer delivering an amazing performance as the witch-woman of Steve's masochistic fantasy.

Isn't She Lovely is trademark Stevie Wonder, a link to every bright and beautiful moment on his records that provides welcome relief from the turgid excess of much of the rest of the album. Written in honor of his daughter Aisha, the song opens with an authentic (uncredited) baby's first cry and proceeds to swing through a melody as smooth and sweet as melted butter. Steve seems to glimpse moments of innocent

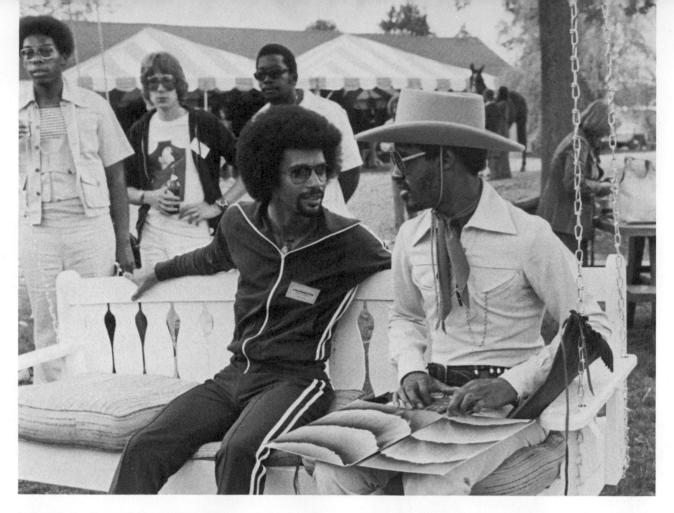

happiness from his earlier days in his vocal performance, thus offering implied corroboration of the premise that his overall message here lacks conviction. The harmonica solo on this track is one of the best things Stevie ever recorded. Like the whole "Key Of Life" project, though, Steve can't resist going on with chorus after chorus here when a fade-out would have undoubtedly strengthened the song. (*Isn't She Lovely* became a top popular song without ever being released as a single.)

Joy Inside My Tears is an incredibly boring six-and-a-half minute dirge that only Stevie's most dedicated fans could find listenable. Emotional pitch can only be sustained for so long before it becomes pointless tedium.

Black Man is the kind of polemic that has always been worth supporting, but seldom makes for enjoyable listening. Steve makes a pointed statement about the importance of non-whites in human (and especially American) history — a laudable sentiment, but tiresome music at eight-minutes-plus. The terse, to-the-point *Living For The City* and *You Haven't Done Nothin'* do so much more to make the point Steve so painfully drives home here over and over. The result, all too often, is that his good intentions are lost, as the impatient listener lifts the needle from the record and goes on to something else. *Black Man* may have been what Steve wanted to say, but it's not going to be on too many people's lists of all-time favorite Stevie Wonder songs.

Ngiculela – Es Un Historia – I Am Singing is a pretty tune sung in three parts and languages to match — Zulu, Spanish and English — with nice synthesizer backgrounds. *If It's Magic* is only an average love song in Steve's catalog, and the pretense of the syrupy harp accompaniment adds nothing to the conviction of the performance.

Wonder has demonstrated the ability to write classic love songs over the years, songs which are often characterized by a disarming simplicity. None of the conviction that inspires such moments is present in the tedious *As*, seven minutes of description about how long his love will last. The list is ridiculous — his love will last until "parrots live at sea" and "eight times eight times eight is four". There are ways to write a seemingly endless variation of love lyrics, but it requires extreme skill, and it's obvious at this point that Stevie's inspiration for this kind of material had dried up, at least temporarily.

Above left: *Stevie relaxing with Ira Tucker, his long-time colleague and personal public relations liaison, during the 1976 launch of "Songs In The Key Of Life" at Longview Farm, Worcester, Massachusetts.*

Another Star closes the proceedings with the Wonderlove band pushing for all they're worth on a charging salsa-influenced song, Bobbi Humphrey guesting on flute while George Benson adds his distinctive guitar accompaniment. This is one track on the album that makes effective use of the longwindedness of the proceedings, building and sustaining intensity through eight minutes without flattening out, unlike so many other songs on "Key Of Life". Unfortunately the mix is poor and Benson's solo in particular suffers as a result.

The bonus EP makes up for some of the disappointment of the rest of the record. *Saturn* is a good ballad about escaping from the evils of earth to an extraterrestrial utopia. Guitarist Mike Sembello co-wrote the song and plays in stately accompaniment to some great Yamaha synthesizer work from Steve.

All Day Sucker is a tremendous Sly Stone-like funk vamp with heavy fuzz guitar from W. G. "Snuffy" Walden, *Ebony Eyes* is one of Steve's better love songs. *Easy Going Evening* signs off with a smooth, relaxed instrumental duet be-

tween harmonicas and synthesizers, with Steve scatting drums behind and Nathan Watts adding bass. The melody is beautiful, and Steve assembles as fine a sequence of harmonica passages as he's every played.

"Songs In The Key Of Life" did feature a handful of outstanding tracks. If the album had been a single disc made up of *Sir Duke, I Wish, Summer Soft, Isn't She Lovely, Another Star, Saturn, All Day Sucker* and *Easy Going Evening*, it would have made an excellent LP, on a par with his previous four classics. As it was, the rest of the material made for ponderous listening, yet the album's strengths were formidable enough to earn Steve the Grammy award for Best Album of the Year, something he'd obviously been counting on, judging from the timing of the record's release. The album came in at No. 1 on *Billboard*'s Top 200 chart, making Stevie the only American artist to achieve such a distinction. *Sir Duke* and *I Wish* went on to be very successful singles. Inexplicably, *Isn't She Lovely* was never released as a single, while *As* and *Another Star* were issued as edited singles.

Above right: *The biggest billboard in America (60 feet high by 270 feet long) in New York City's Times Square reflects the overblown concept of what it advertises: Stevie's 1976 "Songs In The Key Of Life".*

14. Happy Birthday

Though Stevie Wonder didn't tour in support of "Songs In The Key Of Life" during 1977, he stayed active on a number of other fronts. Much of his time was spent in the studio working several projects – a Wonderlove album, his own LP and the soundtrack for a film called *The Secret Life of Plants* (the latter was the only record that came out). He also worked on sessions with Tavares, the Chi-Lites, Peter Frampton, the McRary Singers, Bobbi Humphrey and New Brazil '77. He also did quite a bit of sitting in with other musicians during live shows, including The Commodores, Sarah Dash, Jimmy Smith, Billy Preston, Earth Wind & Fire, the Fania All Stars, Sammy Davis Jr., Nancy Wilson, Lenny White, Elton John and a jam session at Studio 54 in New York with Bobbi Humphrey, George Benson, Steve Stills and Teddy Pendergrass. An appearance with Ella Fitzgerald at the New Orleans Jazz and Heritage Festival was aired on National Public Radio.

In February, 1977 Stevie went to Nigeria to play with local musicians in FESTAC '77, the second world black and African cultural festival. He closed the show on the final night of the festival playing with an African band. Stevie was piped back to the U.S. via satellite tie-in for the Grammy awards, but the hook-up failed: you could see the video signal but there was no audio coming through. Andy Williams made a public blunder at the U.S. end as he pleaded to Stevie in front of a national television audience, "Stevie, can you see us?" Steve went on to collect five Grammys at the event – Album of the Year (artist and producer), Best Producer, Best Male Pop Vocalist and Best R&B Male Vocalist. Steve's personal happiness was enhanced by the birth of his son, Kieta Sawandi, on 16 April. The name is a combination of West and South African words meaning "worshipper" and "founder" respectively.

Steve's twenty-seventh birthday was celebrated with a surprise party arranged by his brother Calvin at Rosy's Restaurant in New Orleans. Calvin asked Stevie to help plan a party for Wonderlove pianist Greg Phillinganes for 12 May. At the stroke of midnight the Trammps (*Disco Inferno*) took the stage and started singing "Happy Birthday To Stevie". The same year Stevie attended a lavish birthday celebration for Aretha Franklin and threw parties for brothers Calvin, Timothy and Milton and sister Renee as well as various members of his office staff. During a small birthday gathering for Yolanda at Copacabana Stevie entertained the audience by singing a few songs accompanied by himself on acoustic piano.

Stevie also continued his charity work, giving a twenty thousand dollar phone pledge to the High Blood Pressure telethon. The most demanding charitable service he had to perform, though, came when he had to talk old friend Lee Garrett out of a suicide attempt in August. "Sheriff's deputies in Los Angeles report that Stevie Wonder, the pop singer, helped talk his former musical composer, Lee Garrett, out of taking his own life," stated the report in *The New York Times*. Garrett had called a suicide hotline, then locked himself in a bathroom for five hours with a gun. Stevie's arrival undoubtedly turned the tide in saving Garrett's life.

When it finally was released, the "Journey Through The Secret Life Of Plants" album proved to be everything "Key Of Life" was supposed to be, a musical evolution into completely new styles that surpassed in scope anything he'd previously done. Stevie had tried to come to terms with a variation on the symphonic form in this soundtrack, and produced a stunning piece of program music in the process. Ironically, "Secret Life" was an abject commercial failure, his poorest reception since "Music Of My Mind", the first album he recorded when he left the Motown production team.

Nevertheless, "Secret Life" was something Steve could be proud of. The stylistic range of the album was impressive, moving from the romantic swells of *Earth's Creation* and *The*

First Garden to the sitar-drenched meditation *Voyage To India*, the spongy funk of *Venus Flytrap And The Bug*, a Japanese children's chorus in *Ai No, Sono*, the semi-disco groove of *Race Babbling*, the stately classical melody of *Ecclesiastes* and the infectious African rhythms of *Kesse Ye Lolo De Ya*. He still managed to include several ballads in his characteristic style – *Black Orchid, Come Back As A Flower*, and *Outside My Window*. Though Wonderlove hadn't toured for quite a while before the album was released, the full band assembled for *A Seed's A Star And Tree Medley*, blasting through an incredibly powerful arrangement that scaled Steve's highest peaks of musical excitement.

The album closes on two spectacular instrumentals, *Tree* and *Finale*, an astoundingly beautiful climax to the record. Steve's touch on a variety of keyboards, particularly his continuing exploitation of Yamaha synthesizer, was given its freest imaginative reign in service of the soundtrack. Even his harmonica work and his singing were unusually intentive – on *Power Flower* his voice, acting out the character of the nature god Pan, is pitched so high it sounds like someone else is singing. Philip Bailey, the Earth, Wind & Fire member who would later go on to solo success with songs like *Easy Lover*, made a comment about the different moods Stevie can evoke. "I was always impressed by Stevie. He has an ability to change characters so that we aren't

Previous page: *Berry Gordy joins Stevie and members of Wonderlove to celebrate Motown's twentieth anniversary in 1980. Even while Stevie began to apply political pressure for a celebration of Martin Luther King's*

birthday with personal appearances like this impromptu
singalong in New York City (above left), he found time
for family life (above). Taking his daughter Aisha to the
Barnum and Bailey circus at Madison Square Garden.

119

bored with one style."

The decision to do a soundtrack was a special challenge for Steve, that resulted from a meeting he'd had with filmmaker Michael Braun several years before. "Braun wanted me to write a song for the closing of the picture," Steve explained, "so I did what was to be called *Tree* on the album. Well, that tune wasn't compatible with the rest of the music someone else already scored for the film, so they asked me to do the whole thing. I didn't really feel comfortable with the idea at first. I felt that I couldn't do it, but then I decided, well, it was a challenge. And, too, the more I heard people ask 'How will Steve, being blind, be able to write music for a film?' the more of a challenge it became. I just knew I'd have to figure out some way to do it.

"So we used the headphones. In the left headphone Michael would explain what was happening in the film visually, and in the right headphone my engineer Gary Olazbal would give me the time of the actual frames. He would tell me the starting time of a sequence and count the frames till it would end. They put it all on this four-track tape; the sound of the film, the sound of Michael explaining, and the sound of Gary counting on three of the tracks; the fourth would be used for the music whenever I finished it. Then they made me a copy, I'd take it home,

listen to it a few times, and work the music out on a tape cassette. I would play along with it, and get the time signature I felt was conducive to the sequence. That's how we did it."

The results were wonderful, and formed the basis for an extraordinary stage presentation of "The Secret Life of Plants" at the Auditorium Theater in Chicago, with a full orchestra supporting Wonderlove, but the ensuing 1979 tour was an economic failure which, combined with the lack of success generated by the album, proved a source of bitter frustration to Steve, as he speculated about the lukewarm response he was getting. "I would have liked to see Cobo Hall *full*," he said of a show in his hometown of Detroit that had failed to sell out. (It was Steve's first tour in five years, so the home-coming was a bitter disappointment to him.) "I have to think why it was not – because enough people did not hear about it in time, or because people from what they had heard did not want to spend the money or go to a performance of that kind or because they hadn't been able to get into 'The Secret Life of Plants'.

"The true meaning of an artist is to be expressive of his art and to be innovative. But a lot of things have been afforded me by the people, so I have to share with them the experiences I have had and am having. When I listen to my work and I realize that certain things are too out, too abstract, I try to make it so that everyone will be able to understand it whether they're young or old.

"But if you don't take a chance in life, then you really cannot move forward. If you're going to sit yourself in one thing that you know is going to work, and just do it over and over, then ultimately people are going to get tired of it anyway. And so if you don't make the change, then there will be a change that someone else will make."

Despite this brave sentiment, Steve was under pressure to produce a hit, although *Send One Your Love* was a successful Top 5 single. Instead of waiting another two years and taking the chance of being forgotten altogether he rushed back into the studio to record another album. Stevie's commercial touch was far from blunted as his incredible production on Jermaine Jackson's *Let's Get Serious* (1980) proved. After almost a year of work and over twenty different sessions working on that one song, Jackson's career was revitalized when it became a huge

Above left: Stevie and the Rolling Stones' Keith Richard buried the hatchet of previous differences at New York's Xenon disco after a concert by Stevie in December 1979.

120

hit. "Hotter Than July" which was released in 1980 (just in time for Motown's twentieth anniversary celebration) was an altogether traditional Stevie Wonder album designed to be accessible to the public and produce hit singles. A full complement of Wonderlovers, including a four piece horn section, kick things off in high spirits with the free swinging *Did I Hear You Say You Love Me*, with great guitar playing from Benjamin Bridges. *All I Do* keeps the same pronounced dance beat going in a clean segue, with Steve playing all the parts except Hank Redd's saxophone. But Steve never surrenders to the lockstep beat, pushing and teasing the rhythm with his singing and keyboard work. The song was originally written in 1966. The background vocals were by the OJs, Michael Jackson and Betty Wright.

Rocket Love, a spacey, Brazilian-flavored medium-tempo ballad, features excellent synthesizer playing from Steve and a sprightly Paul Riser string arrangement. Steve's Benny Benjamin-inspired drumming on *I Ain't Gonna Stand For It* is another one of those amazing moments he just seems to toss off occasionally. The song certainly ranks among his very finest work, a shouting medium for some hot vocals that breaks without a pause into the doubletime tempo of the side's closing dance track, *As If You Read My Mind*, which includes a spirited harmonica solo.

Steve had been playing with reggae musicians and recording a number of reggae tracks for his own benefit throughout most of the seventies and would often delight interviewers with a taste of some of his own brand of dub, but he had never released any reggae music commercially until *Master Blaster (Jammin')*, the tribute to Bob Marley on "Hotter Than July". It's easily the finest track on the record, a great medium for Steve's sophisticated funk, and one can only wonder why he took so long to use the form. The freewheeling *Do Like You* is Steve writing about his kids, revolving around a story about Keita wanting to learn to dance like his sister Aisha, and including both kids in cameo

Above: *Stevie was joined on stage by Diana Ross and Marvin Gaye for a fantastic trio during the Motown Twentieth Anniversary celebrations.*

talking roles that work really well.

Cash In Your Face is a superfunk vamp about the difficulty middle class blacks have finding the kind of housing they want that makes its point without coming across as preachy. *Lately*, the album's only standard Stevie Wonder love ballad, is a beautiful song about one of Steve's favorite subjects over the years, the fear of losing his lover.

The album closes with Steve's homage to the Rev. Dr. Martin Luther King, *Happy Birthday*. The song was designed to be an anthem for the crusade to make King's birthday, 15 January, a national holiday. The repeated choruses of "happy birthday" beautifully express the joy and optimism of the movement.

Wonder campaigned hard for Martin Luther King day. He attended the 1981 parade by Washington's blacks in support of the proposed holiday, and by 1982 he'd become one of the central figures behind the movement. In November 1981 he gave a press conference at the Los Angeles press club to announce the 1982 march, which he had coordinated with King's widow, Coretta Scott King, with Congressman John Conyers, the sponsor of a bill to make King's birthday a national holiday, and District of Columbia Congressman Walter E. Fauntroy.

"To increase the effectiveness of our efforts next year," said Wonder at the press conference, "I contacted Mrs. King, Congressman Conyers and Congressman Fauntroy with a view toward developing a national mobilization strategy and developing a legislative plan that would be compatible with Mrs. King's efforts in Atlanta and the Congressmen's efforts on Capitol Hill. I am pleased that Mrs. King, the black leadership and I have come together to mutually plan how we will be supportive of each other's efforts this year."

On Friday, 15 January, 1982, the people of Washington, D.C. were in a state of shock. The city had been buffeted all week long by a series of snowstorms that had paralyzed local traffic. On the previous Wednesday afternoon an Air Florida jet taking off from National Airport en route to Miami smashed into the Fourteenth Street Bridge between D.C. and the state of Virginia, killing almost all the passengers on board as well as several motorists on the bridge. Only an hour afterwards a major accident oc-

Stevie's powerful performances (left) helped him to become a focus for political interest in the campaign for Martin Luther King Day. Above: *Celebrating his 32nd birthday at an impromptu party at the New York Hilton.*

Stevie roller-skating with friends in New York. He has never allowed his blindness to prevent him from activities that others might consider beyond him.

hotter than *July*."

The audience whistled and applauded at Stevie's reference to the album that included the King Day anthem, *Happy Birthday*.

"Dr. King left an unfinished symphony," Wonder went on, "which we must finish. We must harmonize our notes and chords and create love and life."

Then Wonder gave his pitch for a national day of tribute to Martin Luther King and his message. "We need a day to celebrate our work on an unfinished symphony, a day for a dress rehearsal for our solidarity."

Wonder's speech struck a positive note at a time when the black community in the United States was reeling from setbacks that had threatened to destroy all the gains they had painstakingly made since the mid-fifties. Newly-elected President Ronald Reagan had openly appealed to the nation's most extreme right wing elements in his campaign. Following his election the Ku Klux Klan, the long-standing and most notorious group of anti-black vigilantes, stepped up their activities and resumed the practise of lynching blacks in the South. Reagan campaigned hard to repeal the Voting Rights Act, which had given many southern blacks their first opportunity to vote. Reagan's economic policies seemed calculated to hit the poorest elements of the nation's electorate the hardest. In this desolate atmosphere the militant rhetoric that characterized much black political thinking in the sixties and seventies sounded too much like empty bombast, while Wonder's careful message of hope offered more appropriate spiritual sustenance.

The day after the rally, Wonder was being identified by political journalists as one of the black community's new leaders. "It was Wonder," wrote Herbert Denton in the *Washington Post*, "with his lyrical talk and song about such old-fashioned matters as love, pride and excellence who got deafening cheers and seemed to better understand the yearnings of the legions of youthful marchers who braved the cold for the event yesterday."

Before the rally Wonder had told reporters "I think that the people, young people, are really reaching out for something. It is important for those of us who have positions to respond, to acknowledge the fact that they are reaching out for that kind of oneness, that kind of tenderness."

Denton concluded that "Wonder appeared intuitively to comprehend a bit better than the old-line civil rights groups ... that the assaults on the sense of pride of blacks have been felt as deeply, maybe even more deeply, as the assaults on their pocketbooks".

While Steve had apparently gone into another period of recording inactivity following "Hotter Than July" he intensified his work in the studio with other artists. He had already rescued the flagging career of Jermaine Jackson, and he went on to collaborate with the reggae band Third World on their excellent 1982 hit album, "You've Got The Power".

Steve originally met members of Third World during a 1969 trip to Jamaica, and stayed in contact off and on over the years until July, 1982, when Wonder joined Third World on stage at the Reggae Sunsplash Festival in a tribute to the late Bob Marley, playing Wonder's *Master Blaster (Jammin')* and Marley's *Redemption Song*. Rita Marley also sang on *Redemption Song*. After the show, Wonder proposed that he write and produce some material for the band's next album. The result was the hit single, *Try Jah Love*, and another hot track entitled *They're Playing Us Too Close*.

Third World percussionist Carrot recalls how effortlessly Stevie influenced their recording. "He said 'Hey I have a tune for you'," smiles Carrot, "so we did it. It was time for us to do our album but we were going to do it differently. We went and recorded *Playing Us Too Close* and he wrote another one which was *Try Jah Love*. He came in and he just started playing it, just like that. So we started playing with him and the whole thing grew, we recorded the tune."

"He didn't have all the lyrics that night," explains Carrot. "He went and wrote the lyrics and came back. It was good. We went home and listened to it and it grew on us. Two tunes, slightly different messages, but good tunes. He inspired the album as a whole. He gave us strength to know that he saw fit to associate with us."

Third World was impressed by Wonder's balancing of production and performance skills. "When he plays a tune it's because he doesn't hear anybody else doing it," says Carrot. "He says 'I'd like to express this thought, or this desire, and there's no one else expressing it, so let me do it.' If there was someone else who would express his desires, his thoughts, he would just sit back and produce it. He allows you to express what you feel. He doesn't stifle you. You can hear it in his music. He uses anything that comes to mind, a baby crying, a baby laughing, a baby in a bath, he makes some real primitive sounds with his voice and he's not apologetic about it."

Stevie's most celebrated collaboration that year was with Paul McCartney, guesting on his "Tug Of War" album. Stevie wrote a song for the album, *What's That You're Doing*, as well as sharing vocals on McCartney's composition *Ebony And Ivory*, a children's song promoting international brotherhood.

Wonder recalls the circumstances that led to this meeting of musical minds. "I ran into a gentleman who told me that Paul had written this song and he'd like to get a tape of it to me. I listened to the song and I liked what it was talking about. It politely asked for people to reflect upon life using the terms of music, a piano, a black and white keyboard, and harmony, this melting pot of many different people. It's a great song. I like Paul a lot. I think we have a lot of similar thoughts. I'm happy that we had a chance to meet each other for a greater period of time because it did give me a little more insight on the Beatles, on his feelings, on his life and his person."

It seems strange that Stevie emphasized how closely the song brought the two together since they exchanged most of the collaboration from a distance. Even the music video for the song was shot with Stevie and Paul on two different continents, then cleverly edited to make it appear that they were in the same room when it was made. Critical reaction to *Ebony And Ivory* was almost universally negative — the simple, idealistic message would probably have been accepted from Wonder on his own but the presence of McCartney may have made the thing seem too calculated and perhaps even insincere.

Wonder, however, defends the song to this day. "Lots of times when things are said very clearly it is almost like speaking in the mind of a child," he argues. "Even though I did not write the song, I am and I was in total agreement with what the lyric was saying and because of that I felt it would be right for Paul and me to do that song together. I felt that for whatever significance we both have, both in multi-colored, multi-racial society, we're all many different

colors and cultures, it would be good for us to sing something like that. And so when I was approached to do it I said it would be really good to do it. It was my pleasure, outside of being a fan of his, the fact that we had mutual respect for each other throughout the years. It was a good time and a good song to get that message across, about ebony and ivory."

Unfortunately the attention paid to *Ebony And Ivory*, which became a big hit, detracted from the great *What's That You're Doing?* The song shows both musicians in their best light, pushing and pulling each other instrumentally through a lengthy, exciting track as Steve challenges Paul to some of the finest bass playing he's ever recorded. The two engage in beautiful vocal exchanges with McCartney mimicking Steve's slurred, bluesy diction so closely it's hard to tell which one of them is singing at times. They finish the song with a breathtaking reference to the Beatles' early hit, *She Loves You*.

As successful as his work with others continued to be, Wonder's lack of production on his own led Motown in 1982 to release "The Original Musiquarium", a disguised greatest hits package. The record, made up for the most part of re-mixed material from his seventies albums, includes four new songs — the soft love ballad, *Ribbon In The Sky*, the funky, slyly melodic *That Girl*, a fantastic anti-war rocker called *Front Line* and the ten-minute plus album closing extravaganza, *Do I Do*, recorded with the full band and featuring a trumpet solo from Dizzy Gillespie. Stevie raps at the end as the track winds down.

It's hard to understand completely the logic behind "Musiquarium". Steve certainly has plenty of unreleased material available to fill out a record, but perhaps after the bad experience of "Secret Life Of Plants" he wanted to rely on proven hits. Indeed, "Musiquarium" is a great collection of songs, and the re-mix definitely enhances the quality of some of Steve's best material. Perhaps the answer lies in the fact that Steve signed yet another contract with Motown simultaneous with the release of "Musiquarium", which filled out the conditions of the previous deal. This time there were no glowing speeches about solidarity and no boasts about the amount of money involved in the pact. It has even been suggested that Steve took a bit of a cut relative to the previous deal.

Stevie Wonder and Paul McCartney got together to make the hit single Ebony And Ivory. *The song may have got some bad press but it did help to put across the harmony between races which Stevie is constantly promoting.*

15. Love Light In Flight

"Original Musiquarium" marked the end of an era in Stevie Wonder's work. The record became his final comment on the music that represented his coming-of-age. The decade that began with "Music Of My Mind" and ended with "Hotter Than July" encompasses a body of songwriting that ranks with the most impressive and influential career statements made by any popular music figure in history.

Stevie Wonder dominated the seventies. He almost singlehandedly broke down radio airplay color barriers while articulating a rough edged idealism that characterized the age in simple, forceful lyrics, and pioneering many technological advances in sound manipulation which have since become recording industry staples.

The 1980s posed a new set of difficulties for the man. As an adult in his thirties the time had passed when Stevie could simply breathe life into pop music with fresh ideas and insight. The fast paced trendiness of the entertainment industry ensures that no single figure can rule it indefinitely. The fully mature Stevie Wonder was forced to realize that the mantle of pop royalty which had once fallen onto his shoulders had been passed along.

Only a few years before, Michael Jackson had been part of the precocious vocal backing the Jackson Five added to Stevie's *You Haven't Done Nothing*. By 1983 Michael Jackson had eclipsed Stevie as America's most popular musician and "Thriller" broke the sales-figure records that Stevie had set in the previous decade. The 15-minute "mini-feature" pop video that accompanied the *Thriller* hit single was a significant turning point. Stevie has certainly justified the claim that his blindness is more of a gift than a handicap, but the record industry's preoccupation with the surface images of video is a direction that doesn't exactly work towards his strengths.

These changes have unquestionably posed serious problems for Stevie Wonder. Changing fashions in music making may well have caused uncertainty in his mind about what his public musical direction should be, but it certainly didn't stop him from recording almost nonstop and continuing to stockpile the greatest treasure trove of unreleased material since Jimi Hendrix.

In the midst of this shifting reality, though, you can see Stevie subtly adjusting his persona, carefully avoiding an easy pigeonhole. Where once he had been the finger popping kid, then the uncontrollable rock/funk teenage dynamo, then the visionary genius talent come of age, then the hero back from the dead, Steveland Morris has lifted his pop star status into the realm of a religious figure, teacher, shaman, philosopher, even a kind of spiritual leader.

Acting as if making records were only an incidental part of what he does, in the first half of the eighties Stevie threw his energy into producing, playing and writing songs for other people's records, organizing his own studio and custom label and remaining politically active. His Los Angeles headquarters is a large, multi-million dollar complex housing a state-of-the-art recording studio, countless synthesizers, and a machine that "reads" books electronically for the sightless.

"I'd like to always feel there is going to be something different," Stevie said recently about his recording output. "Quite naturally with the technical advancements that are being made there are a great many things you can do. I have a gentleman who works with me on software programs that interface the various units that I use. The artificial speech synthesizer connects with the output of the various units to give me the information in braille. Or I can use the speech synthesizer as a terminal and write in what I want, getting immediate speech output. It gives me a chance to have what up until recently could only be possible through seeing the visual display." Stevie's program "gentleman" is one of a staff of over 100 people including various relatives and his four brothers, Calvin, Milton, Timothy and Larry Hardaway. He also owns his own radio station, KJLH in Los Angeles.

songs himself and told the crowd, "Sometimes you do these songs and you get back into the situation you experienced and you just can't help yourself."

After a hot version of *Overjoyed* and *Ribbon In The Sky,* Stevie went into one of the show's highlights, a fast paced, slickly arranged medley of *Uptight, For Once In My Life, My Cherie Amour, Signed, Sealed, Delivered, Higher Ground, You Haven't Done Nothin'* and *Living For The City.* Stevie acknowledged that Motown and the rest of the world was waiting for his long anticipated new album and apologized about the delay before launching into yet another new

tune, *Go Home.*

Sir Duke and *I Wish* formed part of another medley, and Stevie did *Do I Do* before bringing on Eddie Murphy and Joe Piscopo and performing a bit of *Love's In Need Of Love Today* at Murphy's request.

Stevie stopped the set and asked for some children to come to the stage. When a number of toddlers came on Stevie started joking with them. "No playing the piano," he mock scolded. "Someone will come out and pull your fingers out." He laughed and went on, "We're gonna sing a song now, it's called *Gimme That Wine,"* and he laughed even harder. "No I'm kidding,"

Stevie in performance at Radio City Music Hall. After a recording silence of some five years it was the soundtrack album for The Woman In Red *(inset) which brought him back into the charts in the mid-eighties.*

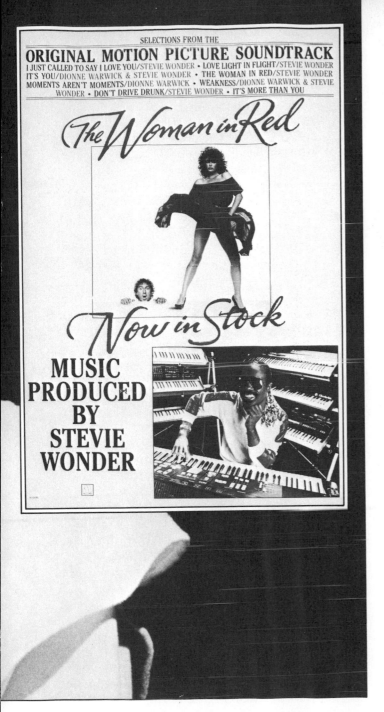
nent of the holiday who had tried a shameful smear campaign against Dr. King in order to appeal to bigoted voters in his home state of South Carolina. When the entire Radio City Music Hall crowd erupted into boos at the mention of Helms, Wonder cautioned: "Every minute you allow yourself to hate, you've wasted one minute God has given you to love."

Before the next show Stevie was able to give a jubilant press conference announcing how pleased he was that the Senate had voted in favor of the King holiday. The holiday would be held nationally on the third Monday in January, starting on 20 January 1986.

Stevie released the following statement, entitled "Somewhere Dr. King Is Smiling":

"Somewhere Dr. King is smiling, not because his birthday is a holiday; but because he, too, is convinced that we are moving in the right direction. I know that Dr. King appreciates that this day is a day for all Americans to celebrate love, peace and unity. It is not the cure-all, but it is a healing aid.

"I'm so happy that America has this holiday! Although it will not be official until 1986, we can begin our celebrations today. Let's celebrate that we have the first holiday that was demanded by the people. Let's celebrate our democratic process that allows us these opportunities. Let's celebrate our collective effort that brought Blacks, Whites, Reds, Browns and Yellows together. Let's celebrate this labor of love. Our new child—A NATIONAL HOLIDAY FOR DR. MARTIN LUTHER KING, JR.

"My overwhelming emotion and objective today is to thank each and every one of the millions of Americans that felt the need for this day. We could never have accomplished this if you didn't have faith in yourself, your country and your fellow Americans. As one of those fellow Americans, I just want to give you a standing ovation and my heartfelt thanks and applause.

That night Stevie and 4,000 people at Radio City Music Hall celebrated in style during *Happy Birthday. Happy Birthday* had always been the anthem of the King holiday campaign, an affirmation of his certainty that they would be successful, "Every time we did the song it was a celebration of that day," said Stevie once the bill had been signed. "I was living its reality every time we performed it. But it wasn't meant to

he continued, then began to play *Ebony And Ivory.* If you ever disliked the song, thought it was too simplistic or banal, it was hard still to feel that way after hearing Stevie sing it with eight little kids picked at random who all knew the words and sang along in a completely spontaneous gesture of universal brotherhood.

The first night of the engagement was the night before the bill sponsoring an official holiday for Martin Luther King was to be voted on in the Senate. In his introduction to *Happy Birthday,* with which he closed the set, Wonder talked about the impending vote and mentioned Senator Jesse Helms, the most outspoken oppo-

brainwash anybody, it was just us living out something that was meant to be."

Wonder took deep satisfaction in winning this political battle. Back in 1981 at the Washington rally on 15 January, Stevie had told the crowd that Dr. King represented the values of peace, love and dignity: "You can assassinate the man but you cannot kill the values." Now in retrospect he insisted that he never doubted the outcome. "I knew that Reagan would sign the bill," Stevie said in a never-before-published interview in 1984. "I told Ira [Tucker, Stevie's personal public relations liaison], 'Didn't I tell you that in '81?' I just knew that. I felt that this was actually the right element for it to actually happen in. No one believed me. Everyone said it was impossible. I just felt that it would happen under this administration. He could have probably gotten a lot more black votes about that whole thing if he had not said something like 'Well, we'll see.' [Laughs.] He was trying to satisfy everybody and he blew himself up. Because it wasn't necessary to say that, but maybe it was for keeping the support of the conservatives. If I were in his campaign, I would say 'Don't say that.' Damn!"

The Radio City shows were part of what Wonder called his "You and Me" tour, a show that later played in Stevie's home town of Detroit and which was taped for cable distribution on the Showtime network in 1984. Speculation about when the new Stevie Wonder album would appear continued well into 1984. Still, attentive fans had already been exposed to a handful of new songs on "Saturday Night Live" and in concert. Some fans were already imagining how the tracks on the new album might be programmed. *Overjoyed, It's Growing* and *Go Home* all seemed to be certainties for the album.

Wonder wrote another song toward the end of March which was soon to cause a controversy. The day after he wrote *Lighting Up The Candles* he discovered that his old friend from the Motown days, Marvin Gaye, had died from gunshot wounds inflicted on the singer by his own father. "It was written about 12 hours before Marvin died," Stevie later said. "I felt something was happening, something was about to go wrong, I didn't know what it was. I thought there was going to be a possible losing of someone. I had gone the night before to see a gentleman who had been a friend, a father, a

brother, he was my musical director and producer for a while, Clarence Paul, who had had a heart attack. I wrote the basic idea of the song and I knew what I wanted to write about. I hadn't finished all the words. I finished the words the night after I went to see Clarence and I went down to the studio and I was sitting at the piano and I finished up the words. That was April Fool's Eve, or the morning, the early morning of April 1. When I was with Clarence at the hospital we were talking and he was saying 'You know I'm tired of record companies, always talking about they've got to have a Michael Jackson or a Marvin Gaye or a Stevie Wonder. We've got to get something new.' I asked him how Marvin was doing and he said 'I talked to him. He seemed to be all right, he was working on his album.' Just in general, we talked about stuff. I told him the last time I'd seen Marvin we were talking about doing this duet thing together, when he was at the Greek theatre. Then I was home the next morning. This guy called me and said 'Marvin Gaye has just been shot.' But I was on another call, I said 'Really?' Before I could get on the line to talk. When you hear things like that, you say, well, this is April Fool's Day, but on the other hand I know he wouldn't be kidding about something like that. But anyway, this song, there was definitely a vibration in the air."

Stevie talked about putting *Lighting Up The Candles* on the next album. "I'd like to, yeah," he said. "But I kind of, I want to do it not as a big choir kind of thing, but more actually than my voice being featured out front, maybe just a little part, and have the rest of it in harmony."

In spite of all the anticipation for the next Stevie Wonder album, few people realized what shape it would actually take. A Gene Wilder comedy, *The Woman In Red,* opened on 15 August, 1984. The film was so-so, but the soundtrack, produced by Stevie Wonder and with several new songs written by him, was great. It was not really promoted as a Stevie Wonder album — the cover features the movie's stock promotional still — and that touch of anonymity was apparently what Stevie needed at the time to spur him on.

The film is actually a pretty stupid situation comedy hooked around sexual fantasy and obsession, animated only by Wilder's comic talents. Stevie is capable of writing love songs in endless variation, though, and his rich imagination actually gave the film more credit than it was due. The result is a soundtrack that explores the limited and banal themes of the film in richly poetic terms that swamp it if you listen carefully.

Stevie Wonder was actually freed by the lack of responsibility to make a record that really represented himself. Writing the soundtrack was merely a project for him, a problem to solve, and he threw his energy into it and came up with a work of astonishing quality. As a result, the album is a curious combination of Wonder's modern sound (created by his total immersion in a studio completely set up to allow him to create one man orchestrations through synthesizer overdubs), and the kind of haphazard collections of songs that characterized his early Motown albums.

With the exception of a few horn and percussion parts and the rhythm section on three tracks, all the music on the album is made by Stevie, and all the songs except one were written by him. Dionne Warwick sings the lead vocal on *Moments Aren't Moments*, sings duets with Stevie on *It's You* and *Weakness*, while Stevie sings the rest. His songs include the throwaway public service announcement, *Don't Drive Drunk*, the funky vamp of a title track, *The Woman In Red*, an exquisite love song, *I Just Called To Say I Love You* and a classic Wonder composition, *Love Light In Flight*. Though the song is tied to Wilder's sexual longing for Kelly Le Brock in the film, it has that under-the-skin universality that Wonder can pull off so effortlessly. Hooked on one of his unforgettable melodic twists and powered by a corkscrewing rhythmic pulse, *Love Light In Flight* becomes as much a song about spirituality as sex, and thus anticipates 1985's *In Square Circle*.

Wilder, who wrote, directed and starred in the movie, didn't get involved with Stevie's soundtrack until the picture was well underway. "At first I thought it would be nice to have two songs, maybe three, and they should contrast inordinately with the romantic background music," he said. "Dionne [Warwick], who's a friend, came to see a middle cut of the film and said: 'Would you mind if I came back and brought Stevie Wonder to see it?'"

Wilder may have been surprised by this request, but Dionne knew about Wonder's passion for going to the movies, where whoever was with him was charged with describing the action scene by scene. Warwick brought Wonder down and gave a running account of the action, after which Stevie asked for a cassette of the dialogue and began work.

"Three days later he'd written two songs," said Gene Wilder, "and played them over the phone to me. Then he wrote one more and I thought that was it. I went to France to relax for a week. Then I got a call at 2 am. It was Dionne saying Stevie wanted to write more."

Stevie recalls his excitement at working out the complete film score. "Dionne Warwick brought the whole story to me," he said. "She was coordinating the music for the film. She told me that it was a Gene Wilder film and I had seen Gene Wilder in some things with Richard Pryor and older movies on television, and I liked its kind of soft and still clean enough sense of humor. The subject matter, what he was dealing with, was something that I know many people can relate to, the story of the film. It was fun to do. It started out with me just doing one song for the film, then I said well I'll do two songs, three songs, then I started talking to Motown about a whole album. Of course they didn't want to hear that because they were waiting for my next album. So I said 'Come on, let's see.' They listened in and liked the stuff. They said 'You know, Stevie, that song *I Just Called To Say I Love You*, that's a great number, that's a smash.' I had told them I wanted to release *It's You* as the first single because I didn't want for me to have done this and have nothing for Dionne. From the standpoint of songs, I thought *I Just Called ...* was a better song. It's a song that I had held for a long time. I wrote that seven years ago, but I just wrote the lyric to the song recently. I had the chorus and the verses back then, but not the body of the song."

Not all the songs on the *Woman In Red* soundtrack were written specifically for the album. "I wrote *Don't Drive Drunk* right before I had a chance to see the movie," Stevie said. "I had seen a lot of commercials about it and I wanted to write a song about it. I think I wrote *Don't Drive Drunk* about two days after Marvin died. After seeing the film I thought 'This would be great in the scene where the guy's in the car and he's driving crazy and he's giving the guy the impression that he's really upset because his woman left him and the whole bit.' So I just put that song in there."

Stevie also admits a certain particular fondness for *Love Light In Flight*. "Sometimes I try to listen to myself as if I were the person who buys the record. I would have to get a good feeling about it. It's a tricky thing because you have to be always objective. You can't be so objective, though, that you let go of feelings. A song like *Love Light In Flight*, I wanted to make it a performance vocal, but also that the emotion would come out. So I really had to listen as if I were listening to enjoy it, not just to criticize it. I had to listen to that vocal as if I were listening to Stevie and I wanted to enjoy him. I wanted to get a feel out of the song, talking about the passion of the lyric."

I Just Called To Say I Love You became a massive hit in the latter half of 1984. It became Stevie's first Number 1 hit in the States since 1977, and his first-ever Number 1 as a solo artist in the U.K. "It's better to wait and get it than never to get it," he told Terry Wogan in December 1985 on the popular British chat show "Wogan". This was another first — he had never before appeared live on U.K. television.

I Just Called... was later nominated for both a Grammy award and an Oscar, but its Oscar eligibility was jeopardized by Stevie's statement that it had been written seven years earlier — only songs written during the year preceding the award are potential Oscar candidates. Stevie cleared up the problem by explaining that only part of the song had already been written and that it was completed specifically for use in *The Woman In Red*. Though it didn't win the Grammy award, *I Just Called To Say I Love You* did eventually win the Oscar.

The unexpected success of "The Woman In Red" as a soundtrack album and *I Just Called To Say I Love You* as a hit single allowed Stevie to relax about his forthcoming album. He was off the hook — whatever he came out with would be compared to "The Woman In Red" rather than "Innervisions" or "Songs In The Key Of Life", and any questions about his commercial abilities were put to rest when *I Just Called...* became one of 1984's biggest hits. In this more favorable climate, Wonder broke his silence about the forthcoming album and took the opportunity to make a couple of political observations as well in an interview at the Carlyle Hotel on 29 October, 1984.

In a little more than a week Ronald Reagan would be elected to his second term as President of the United States. Polls showed Reagan with an insurmountable lead at this point, but Wonder still expressed his concern about the situation. "I was impressed with Geraldine Ferraro in that debate she had with Bush," Wonder said. "But I was probably also impressed with the whole thing of her being from New York because she had that aggressive attitude. And I just don't know how much America is really ready for that, even though I think in one sense the women of this country say they are, and in another sense, I don't know."

When it was pointed out that he seemed very concerned about the election's outcome, Stevie agreed. "Yeah, I'm concerned. I'm concerned because I can see how Reagan can win lots of people over. He's a great actor I think and I think some of his positions based on what we don't know and based on what we do know seem very strong. I'm impressed with what Mondale is talking about because it sounds very real. I think to a certain degree if you breathe the spirit of we've got to have more strength, we've got to have more missiles, we've got to have more sites, we've got to do this to be a strong America, it only breeds for the other side to say the same thing.

"I'm concerned about the arms race and also I think the swing to a great conservatism. Because we're still dealing with the whole question of the equal rights amendment and all that kind of stuff, which to me is a joke in a society, in a country that is supposed to be a melting pot like this, supposed to be a land of the free and the brave. We're still dealing with issues like that. We're still dealing with South Africa, we're still dealing with apartheid. We're still giving them support with various businesses in South Africa. We still are trying to put a freeze to the general public as to what is actually going on in South Africa.

"Maybe that's why I was so impressed with Jesse Jackson when he went over to the Middle East, because the point is whatever people wanted to say about it, and people had a lot to say about it — people in the music industry, people in the press, media, the whole bit — I was impressed because he did it, you see. He *did* it. And it worked. It's important. You've got to say, look, I can't worry about what this person thinks about that. If this is what I feel in here [he points

to his heart], I've got to do it."

Stevie had become confident enough with the material for the forthcoming album that he was able to admit that the biggest problem facing him was to decide which of the many songs he'd written to include. "We've been going back and forth as to should it be a double or a single album. I would like for it to be a double, but I understand that economically things are not the way that maybe they were when people felt okay about buying a double album. That isn't to say that people won't buy a double album, but it is something to be considered far more than maybe before. And I wonder sometimes if people get a chance to really listen to all the

material. Sometimes you can put a lot out there and there are basic things that they will respond to, four or five things that they really like, and you've got sixteen things in there; maybe it's better to put four or five plus some other things that also will get the listening time.

"I've got about 22 songs already. Some of the things that I've done were spread over the last year and a half. I will either revive them to make them sound updated a little bit more or I will write a couple of more things and not use some of the ones I already have.

"If I just do a single album, it has to be no more than ten songs, if that many. I would prefer to do a double only because of the subject

Stevie greets the legendary Lena Horne, during a comeback concert series she gave during 1985.

matter of a story that is in the album. But it will come in two parts instead of one, there will be a part one and a part two. It will be good for what I want to do from a visual standpoint, the use of videos, and it could be good because it gives a person the chance to digest the first part and get ready for the second part. They have movie sequels, so it will be that kind of feel."

Though Wonder has continued to use the approach of recording virtually all the album's parts himself, he did talk about a couple of other musicians he planned to use, musicians from the world of jazz. "I'm going to use Wynton Marsalis [trumpet] and Stan Getz [saxophone] on a song. They're going to record on it. The track is already done." He also showed that he is well aware of the importance of video, and that his political involvement shows no sign of diminishing. "There's a possible video that I want to do, I want to use John Travolta in it. There's a song that I wrote that I'll probably put on the next album, either on the first or second part, that possibly will be adopted as a song for peace by the United Nations. It's called *Rise Everybody*. I did it at the Peace Sunday they had in Los Angeles at the Rose Bowl."

1984-85 had been an intensely productive period for Stevie Wonder. After doing the "Woman In Red" soundtrack album, Wonder also did sessions for several other 1984 releases. He added a harp solo to the King Sunny Ade track *Ase* for the "Aura" album, and also added harmonica solos to the title track of Chaka Khan's "I Feel For You" and on Dizzy Gillespie's "Closer To The Source". Stevie's great musical adaptability explains how he could switch so easily from a jazz session to African music to popular R&B.

It seems as if Stevie Wonder opens up just as he's finishing one of his own projects to work furiously with a host of other musicians around the time of his own record's release. In 1985, while he prepared his first full album of new material in five years, Stevie Wonder seemed to be everywhere. As usual he appeared on a handful of other people's albums, including Rockwell's *She's A Cobra* from the Motown LP "Captured", the *Upset Stomach* track on the soundtrack of *Berry Gordy's The Last Dragon*, and the opening track, *Feel It* on the British trio Feelabilia's debut record.

Stevie also wrote two tracks for Eddie Murphy's first musical album, "How Could It Be".

For the most part the record is a pretty mixed affair, but Wonder's *Do I* and *Everything's Coming Up Roses* are solid songs and Stevie makes sure the performance is right in both cases, so Murphy comes off at least sounding a little better on those two tracks. Wonder also appears on the Eurythmics' album, "Be Yourself Tonight", adding a harmonica part to *There Must Be An Angel (Playing With My Heart)*.

Perhaps the moment that best exemplifies Wonder's character was his contribution to the USA for Africa production, *We Are The World*. The song was written by Lionel Richie and Michael Jackson and the choir assembled to sing it featured an impressive cross section of the country's biggest music stars, but somehow Stevie Wonder's spirit permeates the whole thing. Though Quincy Jones produced the song, on the behind-the-scenes documentary, *The Making Of We Are The World*, you can see how important Stevie's role was in working out the complex vocal arrangements. Wonder is ubiquitous, seated at his piano, offering suggestions, encouragement and criticism. One particularly telling moment shows Wonder actually coaching Bob Dylan, telling him how to sing his part. Jones wanted a special performance from Dylan but it took Wonder to pull that effort out of him. "I just basically was saying 'I have a lot of respect for you,'" Stevie modestly recalled. "More so to just loosen things up, which it did." What exactly was Wonder trying to get out of Dylan? "Almost like kind of a minister part. It's very unique." Wonder's duet section with Bruce Springsteen is the high point of the vocal performance of *We Are The World*.

Wonder's political agenda didn't stop with the approval of a national holiday for Martin Luther King Jr. or the *We Are The World* project. He's become one of the strongest opponents of the segregationist policy of apartheid in South Africa. In February 1985 Wonder joined the non-violent protesters picketing the South African embassy in Washington, D.C., and like many other celebrities and others who joined in the protest he was arrested and briefly held in custody as a symbol of his commitment to the cause: "They said I was disturbing the peace. I was singing."

On 25 March Stevie was awarded an Oscar for best movie song with *I Just Called To Say I Love You*. In his acceptance speech at the Academy

Award ceremonies, Wonder accepted the award "in the name of Nelson Mandela", the imprisoned black South African who has been one of the leading voices against apartheid and is an official "banned person" by the South African government. In response to the statement, South Africa's government-owned broadcasting company announced that it would no longer play Wonder's music over its airwaves. On 13 May, Stevie's 35th birthday, the United Nations Special Committee Against Apartheid held a special meeting to commend Wonder for his work. The committee said the occasion would honor "Wonder's opposition to racial discrimination and, in particular, to apartheid".

Wonder's political commitment is extending beyond the clear objectives of human rights in South Africa. He obviously sees himself as having a mission to get people involved. "I'm very happy now that people are rallying around causes that are against things that have been sicknesses in the system of mankind", he told Mick Brown of the *Sunday Times* during his December 1985 visit to London to promote "In

Square Circle". "Look at AIDS: when people realize life is in jeopardy all the prejudices go out of the window. It's the same with color prejudice, the greed for political power, the nuclear question—they're all sicknesses. The only difference between a bomb and a disease is the time it takes to kill people."

At the Motown television tribute to New York City's Apollo Theater, Wonder once again seemed everywhere, guiding, coaxing, directing, offering tireless enthusiasm for a project honoring the most important venue for black American music in history. The tribute to the big bands segment was a vital part of the show and was launched by Wonder playing *Sir Duke,* his elegant tribute to Duke Ellington. At another point in the show Wonder was joined on stage by Boy George and the two sang *Part Time Lover* together, backed by a chorus of some of Motown's legends. Boy George has obviously been strongly influenced by Wonder's vocal style, but the moment could have been terribly awkward were it not for Wonder's uncanny knack for relaxing everyone around him and

lishers) Golden Note Award. In a short speech Stevie compared record retailers to Santa's helpers for musicians. He went on to talk about the ban on his music in South Africa, saying he didn't mind it at all. "We have the right to dedicate our music," he said, "so mega-ban me! It was proven years ago that being physically blind is no crime, but being spiritually blind is a serious handicap."

Wonder went on to play five songs for the assembly – *Part Time Lover, Broken Glass, Whereabouts, Land of La-La* and *Go Home.*

When "In Square Circle" finally came out in September of 1985, however, only four of the five songs previewed at the NARM convention were on the album. "In Square Circle" revolves around twin themes of love and spiritual politics, dovetailing the interests enough to keep the themes related. For Wonder love is often elevated to a spiritual level anyway – he includes a Dylanesque essay, co-written with Theresa Cropper, in the album package to explain his concept.

The essay outlines Wonder's metaphysical observation that the phrase "In Square Circle" describes a basic mystery of life. "Their hearts were recalling the cycles of love, while their minds were exploring the square root of the universe," wrote Wonder. The essay goes on to explain each of the album's songs in terms of a Socratic argument between truth seekers and an omnipotent philosopher called "Songlife" who is identified as the Cosmic Carrier.

While it's interesting to see some of Wonder's most abstract ideas put down on paper in essay form, you hardly need a guide book to enjoy the songs on "In Square Circle". *Part Time Lover,* a frank account of an illicit affair, is one of the best songs about the shifting passions of love Wonder's ever written. Powered by an irresistible dance music rhythmic groove, the tune completes Wonder's reclamation of his reputation after several years of silence. If *I Just Called ...* proved that Wonder hadn't lost his hit touch for ballad material, *Part Time Lover* showed that he can still write a killer uptempo track, one in fact that ranks with Motown's all-time classics. The tune is strongly reminiscent of the Supremes' *You Can't Hurry Love.*

I Love You Too Much is a happy-go-lucky tune that turns on some of Wonder's most inventive synthesizer playing and could have easily fit on "Innervisions". *Whereabouts* is a tearjerker

subtly exercising complete control of the situation.

Part Time Lover, which would become the first single from "In Square Circle", had been played in public once before, at the NARM convention for record merchandisers and manufacturers in late March. Wonder gave a concert for that organization at the Diplomat Hotel in Hollywood, Florida.

The show was meant to be a preview of "In Square Circle" and was prefaced by two awards which were presented to Stevie, the NARM (National Association of Record Merchandisers) Artist of the Decade Award and the ASCAP (American Society of Composers and Pub-

Above left: *Stevie shows off his "Oscar" after winning the award for Best Original Song with* I Just Called To Say I Love You *in March 1985.* Above right: *Stevie plays for the United Nations Special Committee Against Apartheid*

ballad in which Stevie laments the loss of part of his identity in an old love relationship. *Stranger On The Shore Of Love* is an easy swinging number that once again demonstrates Stevie's adept one-man-band approach and builds to a beautiful sing-along chorus. *Never In Your Sun* is an intriguing song about a lover who only comes to offer solace in the darkest moments, then leaves when things are all right. This is an example of the finely sliced sentiment Wonder is capable of producing in order to write a seemingly endless variation of love songs.

Though most of the reviews of "In Square Circle" described the record as a side of love songs and a side of political songs, Side Two

includes two more songs written to lovers. *Overjoyed* is the by now standard Wonder approach to celebrating the high point of a relationship. In his inimitable style Wonder is so transported as he sings *Overjoyed* that the song sounds more like a religious hymn than a ballad written to a woman. On the other hand, *Go Home* is the kind of tortured self-recrimination that is the emotional flip side of Wonder's vision of love. For every high he expresses there are equally low moments of disappointment and betrayal. In an interesting twist here Wonder accuses himself of the betrayal for a change, telling his true love to go home and realizing too late, after he's lost everything else, that she was

(watched by the Chairman, Major General Joseph N Galba of Nigeria). In May 1985 Stevie was given a special commendation by the committee for his work against apartheid.

the one he really wanted.

Much has been made of *Land Of La La*, but it really seems that aside from the slick groove the song cuts, this comment on Wonder's adopted home town of Los Angeles is a decidedly minor composition for him, far inferior to a great song like *Living For The City*. Similarly, *Spiritual Walkers* is unlikely to make too many people's lists of all-time great Stevie Wonder songs, unless, of course, they happen to be Jehovah's Witnesses. Perhaps it's Michael Jackson's embrace of this apocalyptic religion that makes Wonder write a blatant piece of propaganda for the itinerant evangelists who go door-to-door in their missionary zeal to tell everyone that the end of the world is coming next Friday at 4:30 in the afternoon.

If Wonder's powers flag on those tracks, they're flying high on one of the best "message" songs he's ever written, the brilliant *It's Wrong (Apartheid)*. At his best, one of Wonder's most overwhelming talents is the ability to make a very simple statement ring like a hammer head connecting with a nail, and that's exactly what he does on *It's Wrong*, which may not become the anthem that *Happy Birthday* has done, but will certainly clock in a close second.

Though Wonder dedicated the album "To Marvin and all who we have lost since the beginning of this project", and reproduced a verse of *Lighting Up The Candles* in the sleeve notes, that song is conspicuously absent from "In Square Circle", as are *Broken Glass* (previewed as part of the album at the NARM convention), the song for peace *Rise Everybody* and *It's Growing*, which Stevie played live a couple of times. You can be sure with unreleased material like that sitting around on the shelf it won't be another five years before we get to hear that sequel to "In Square Circle".

By the way, here's some food for thought: *Part Time Lover* became Stevie's 26th top ten hit on Billboard's Hot 100. Only two artists have had more top ten hits. Elvis Presley had 38; the Beatles had 33. Even more amazing is Wonder's consistency. He's had at least one top ten hit single in all but six of the last 23 years.

Stevie Wonder is a dominant cultural figure in contemporary society. For all his accomplishments as musician, singer, composer, arranger and bandleader, Wonder is not merely pop music's "renaissance man". His work and its impact must be measured outside the realms of what is conventionally thought of as the pop world. By the time he was 30, Wonder had abolished the distinction between music as a reflection of mass culture and as a purely personal expression of the musician. He was the biggest-selling artist in Motown's history, yet at the same time a musician at the cutting edge of progressive and experimental new musics.

Wonder also acts as a kind of religious leader to his followers. His moral authority and intense spirituality have been evident ever since he began to record albums reflecting his private visions in the early seventies. Now, at the age of 36 Wonder has been declared the unofficial leader of America's black community. But Wonder's influence, just as it swamps the ordinary spheres inhabited by the entertainer, also cuts across racial and ethnic boundaries. Stevie Wonder is not merely a leader for blacks (or whites). He is a true world leader, a profound spiritual influence.

On Monday, 20 January 1986, the first U.S. holiday honoring the Rev. Dr. Martin Luther King was celebrated. That night, Stevie Wonder hosted a nationally televised gala featuring performances by a host of celebrities including Bill Cosby, Quincy Jones, Eddie Murphy, Yoko Ono, Cyndi Lauper, Dick Gregory, Joan Baez, Diana Ross and Elizabeth Taylor. King's dream had been realized at least to the point where the entire country was given the opportunity to set time aside to applaud his achievements.

However, as many commentators noted at the time, there are still aspects of Dr. King's dream which remain unfulfilled. Indeed, the Ku Klux Klan was painfully conspicuous in its open opposition to the celebrations, while the alienation of young blacks — described as an "underclass" by black activists themselves — continues. Nevertheless, the fact of the celebration has been a major boost to black self-esteem, which has been systematically undermined by the Reagan administration. It focused attention on the institutional racism still rooted in American society and proved, in spite of blatant bandwagoning by President Reagan himself, that black people can turn the tide of events by concerted action. Stevie Wonder has done as much as anyone to make this possible. Now he's going to set about the task of making the rest of Dr. King's dream come true.

Top right: During Motown's TV tribute to the Apollo Theatre in Harlem, Boy George joined forces with Stevie in a duet of Part-Time Lover, *backed by a chorus of Motown legends.*

Above: *Clive Davis, President of Arista Records, Gladys Knight, Burt Bacharach, Carole Bayer Sagher, Dionne Warwick, Stevie and Liz Taylor sing* That's What Friends Are For *in January 1986, for the Foundation to Fight AIDS.*

STEVIE PRESENTS "MOTOWN-MINI"

Stevie, Plaque, Winner and Prize.

THE "MOTOWN MINI" competition, which was organised by EMI records, has been won by 36-year-old Bert Smith, of Rayleigh, Essex.

Bert was the guest of honour at a reception held at the EMI offices in London last Tuesday. He was presented with the first prize, a red BMC Mini de luxe, by Stevie Wonder. Tony Blackburn was also on hand with a few of his "better jokes".

The car has been fitted with a radio and tape recorder. In the boot there were all the albums in the present Tamla Motown series, which were released earlier this year. Bert was also presented with a souvenir plaque specially engraved with autographs of all the Tamla Motown artistes.

Fifteen thousand entries were received for the competition, which asked entrants to select the twelve tracks from 20 given, they thought should be included on the next "British Motown Chartbusters" album. They were also asked to write a short slogan giving the reasons for the choice.

Bert found the entry form for the competition inside the Diana Ross and the Supremes' album, "Love Child". He was in London with his wife on a shopping spree, shortly after the birth of their third daughter, Joady. They spotted the album in an Oxford Street store and decided it would be nice to have it in their collection, to celebrate the birth of little Joady.

After the presentation of the Mini, Bert was asked how he came to make the winning choice of songs.

"It was sheer luck," he smiled. "When we got home we filled in the form in the same way as we would do the football pools — with a pin! I still can't believe it, you know. The only thing I have ever won before was a bottle of Scotch, and that was a long time ago."

Bert, who has been driving a 1955 Morris Oxford which he bought for £50 three years ago, added: "It will be great to have a car that does not rattle!"

The car was supplied by Kenning Car Mart Ltd. The dealer's prize of a television set went to Mr. Ken Whitmarsh of the H.M.V. store in Oxford Street, London.

Tony Blackburn, President of the Tamla Appreciation Society talks to Stevie.

Songwriter:A:Dylan; B:Moy/Wonder/Cosby
Producer:A:Paul; B:Paul/Cosby
Released:June 1966 (US); August 1966 (UK) .
Reached number 9 US Pop charts; number 1 US R & B charts

A:*A Place In The Sun*

B:*Sylvia*
US Tamla 54139; UK Tamla Motown TMG 588
Songwriter:A:Miller/Wells; B:Moy/Cosby
Producer:A:Paul; B:Cosby
Released:October 1966 (US); December 1966 (UK)
Reached number 9 US Pop charts; number 3 US R & B charts; number 20 UK charts

A:*Someday At Christmas*
B:*The Miracles Of Christmas*
US Tamla 54142
Songwriter:Miller/Wells
Producer:Cosby
Released:November 1966 (US)

A:*Travelin' Man*
B:*Hey Love*
US Tamla 54147; UK Tamla Motown TMG 602
Songwriter:A:Miller/Wells; B:Paul/Broadnax/Wonder
Producer:Paul
Released:February 1967 (US); April 1967 (UK)

A:*I Was Made To Love Her*
B:*Hold Me*
US Tamla 54151; UK Tamla Motown TMG 613
Songwriter:A:Cosby/Hardaway/Wonder/Moy; B:Paul/Broadnax/Wonder
Producer:A:Cosby; B:Cosby/Paul/Stevenson
Released:May 1967 (US); June 1967 (UK)
Reached number 2 US Pop charts; number 1 US R & B charts; number 5 UK charts

A:*I'm Wondering*
B:*Every Time I See You I Go Wild*
US Tamla 54157; UK Tamla Motown TMG 626
Songwriter:Moy/Wonder/Cosby
Producer:Cosby
Released:September 1967 (US); October 1967 (UK)
Reached number 12 US Pop charts

A:*Shoo-Be-Doo-Be-Doo-Da-Day*
B:*Why Don't You Lead Me To Love*
US Tamla 54165; UK Tamla Motown TMG 653
Songwriter:Moy/Wonder/Cosby
Producer:Cosby
Released:March 1968 (US); April 1968 (UK)
Reached number 9 US Pop charts; number 1 US R & B charts

A:*You Met Your Match*
B:*My Girl*
US Tamla 54168; UK Tamla Motown TMG 666
Songwriter:A:Hunter/Wonder/Hardaway; B:Robinson/White
Producer:A:Hunter/Wonder; B:Cosby
Released:July 1968 (US); August 1968 (UK)

A:*For Once In My Life*
B:*Angie Girl*

US Tamla 54174; UK Tamla Motown TMG 679
Songwriter:A:Miller/Murden; B:Moy/Wonder/Cosby
Producer:Cosby
Released:October 1968 (US); November 1968 (UK)
Reached number 2 US Pop charts; number 2 US R & B charts; number 3 UK charts

A:*I Don't Know Why*
B:*My Cherie Amour*
US Tamla 54180; UK Tamla Motown TMG 690
Songwriter:A:Riser/Hunter/Wonder/Hardaway; B:Moy/Wonder/Cosby
Producer:A:Hunter/Wonder; B:Cosby
Released:February 1969 (US); March 1969 (UK)
Reached number 4 US Pop charts; number 4 US R & B charts; number 14 UK charts

A:*Yester-Me, Yester-You, Yesterday*
B:*I'd Be A Fool Right Now*
US Tamla 54188; UK Tamla Motown TMG 717
Songwriter:A:Miller/Wells; B:Moy/Wonder/Cosby
Producer:A:Fuqua/Bristol; B:Cosby
Released:October 1969 (US); November 1969 (UK)

148

Reached number 1 in US Pop charts; number 5 US R & B charts; number 2 UK charts

A:*Never Had A Dream Come True*
B:*Somebody Knows, Somebody Cares*
US Tamla 54191; UK Tamla Motown
TMG 731
Songwriter:Moy/Wonder/Cosby
Producer:A:Cosby; B:Wonder/Hunter
Released:January 1970 (US); March
1970 (UK)
Reached number 26 US Pop charts; number
6 UK charts

A:*Signed, Sealed, Delivered (I'm Yours)*
B:*I'm More Than Happy (I'm Satisfied)*
US Tamla 54196; UK Tamla Motown
TMG 744
Songwriter:A:Hardaway/Wright/Wonder/
Garrett; B:Moy/Wonder/Cosby/Grant
Producer:A:Wonder; B:Cosby
Released:June 1970 (US); June 1970 (UK)
Reached number 3 US Pop charts; number 1
US R & B charts; number 15 UK charts

A:*Heaven Help Us All*
B:*I Gotta Have A Song*
US Tamla 54200; UK Tamla Motown
TMG 757
Songwriter:A:Miller;
B:Wonder/Hunter/Hardaway/Riser
Producer:A:Miller/Baird; B:Hunter/Wonder
Released:October 1970 (US); October
1970 (UK)
Reached number 9 US Pop charts; number 2
US R & B charts

A:*We Can Work It Out*
B:*Never Dreamed You'd Leave In
Summer*
US Tamla 54202
Songwriter:A:Lennon/McCartney;
B:Wonder/Wright
Producer:Wonder
Released:March 1971 (US)
Reached number 13 US Pop charts

A:*We Can Work It Out*

B:*Don't Wonder Why*
UK Tamla Motown TMG 772
Songwriter:A:Lennon/McCartney; B:Caston
Producer:Wonder
Released:May 1971 (UK)

A:*Never Dreamed You'd Leave In
Summer*
B:*If You Really Love Me*
UK Tamla Motown TMG 779
Songwriter:Wonder/Wright
Producer:Wonder
Released:July 1971 (UK)

A:*If You Really Love Me*
B:*Think Of Me As Your Soldier*
US Tamla 54208; UK Tamla Motown
TMG 798
Songwriter:Wonder/Wright
Producer:Wonder
Released:August 1971 (US); January
1972 (UK)
Reached number 8 US Pop charts; number 4
US R & B charts; number 20 UK charts

A:*What Christmas Means To Me*
B:*Bedtime For Toys*
US Tamla 54214
Songwriter:A:Cosby/Gaye/Story;
B:Miller/Murden
Producer:Cosby
Released:December 1971 (US)

A:*Superwoman (Where Were You When I
Needed You)*

B:*I Love Every Little Thing About*
US Tamla 54216
Songwriter:Wonder
Producer:Wonder
Released:May 1972 (US)

A:*Superwoman*
B:*Seems So Long*
UK Tamla Motown TMG 827
Songwriter:Wonder
Producer:Wonder
Released:September 1972 (U

A:*Keep On Running*
B:*Evil*

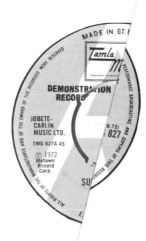

My Ernestine Pearce...

HOW long can one man continue to churn out hit after hit? Is there a limit on genius? Since 1963, Stevie Wonder's voice has dropped, his style has changed, he's learned to play every instrument imaginable and grown in all directions — mostly up.

All these alterations, yet the Stevie Wonder of now is relentless in his production of top ten hits all over the world. Following the monumental success of "For Once In My Life" (which surely must rank alongside of Webb's "By The Time I Get To Phoenix" as one of the most widely-covered songs ever). Stevie celebrates an important event in view by reaching an amazing number three in this week's charts.

What's so important? Only his coming marriage to the lovely Ernestine Pearce of the Flirtations. And his chart-busting record. Miss Pearce became Stevie's betrothed during his last British ... did he have his mind on the music? Only Ernestine knows for sure. At any rate, Stevie has always been a fan of large families, so Motown agents will be having their eyes peeled. Title of the record: "My Cherie Amour". Above: Stevie with Ernestine

Reached number 1 US Pop charts; number 1 US R & B charts

A:*Sir Duke*
B:*Tuesday Heartbreak*
UK Motown TMG 1068
Songwriter:Wonder
Producer:Wonder
Released:March 1977 (UK)
Reached number 2 UK charts

A:*Another Star*
B:*Creepin'*
US Tamla 54286; UK Motown TMG 1083
Songwriter:Wonder
Producer:Wonder
Released:August 1977 (US); August 1977 (UK)

A:*As*
B:*Contusion*
US Tamla 54291; UK Motown TMG 1091
Songwriter:Wonder
Producer:Wonder
Released:November 1977 (US); November 1977 (UK)

A:*Send One Your Love*
B:*(Instrumental)*
US Tamla 54303; UK Motown TMG 1149
Songwriter:Wonder

Producer:Wonder
Released:October 1979 (US); November 1979 (UK)
Reached number 4 US Pop charts

A:*Black Orchid*
B:*Blame It On The Sun*
UK Motown TMG 1173
Songwriter:A:Wonder; B:Wonder/Wright
Producer:Wonder
Released:January 1980 (UK)

A:*Outside My Window*
B:*Same Old Story*
US Tamla 54308; UK Motown TMG 1179
Songwriter:Wonder
Producer:Wonder
Released:March 1980 (US); March 1980 (UK)

A:*Masterblaster (Jammin')*
B:*Masterblaster* (Dub)
US Tamla 54317; UK Motown TMG 1204
Songwriter:Wonder
Producer:Wonder
Released:September 1980 (US); September 1980 (UK)
Reached number 5 US Pop charts; number 1 US R & B charts; number 2 UK charts

A:*I Ain't Gonna Stand For It*
B:*Knocks Me Off My Feet*
US Tamla 54320; UK Motown TMG 1215
Songwriter:Wonder
Producer:Wonder
Released:December 1980 (US); December 1980 (UK)
Reached number 11 US Pop charts; number 10 UK charts

A:*Lately*
B:*If It's Magic*

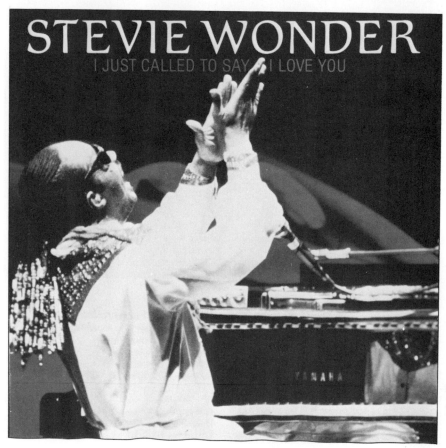

US Tamla 54323; UK Motown TMG 1226
Songwriter:Wonder
Producer:Wonder
Released:April 1981 (US); March 1981 (UK)
Reached number 3 UK charts

A:***Did I Hear You Say You Love Me***
B:***As If You Read My Mind***
US Tamla 54328
Songwriter:Wonder
Producer:Wonder
Released:July 1981 (US)

A:***Happy Birthday***
B:***Happy Birthday Singalong***
UK Motown TMG 1235
Songwriter:Wonder
Producer:Wonder
Released:July 1981 (UK)
Reached number 2 UK charts

A:***That Girl***
B:***All I Do***
US Motown T – 1602F
Songwriter:A:Wonder;
B:Wonder/Paul/Broadnax
Producer: Wonder
Released:January 1982 (US)
Reached number 4 US Pop charts; number 1
US R & B charts

A:***Do I Do***
B:***Rocket Love***
US Motown T – 1612F
Songwriter:Wonder
Producer:Wonder
Released:May 1982 (US); May 1982 (UK)
Reached number 13 US Pop charts; number
1 US R & B charts; number 10 UK charts

A:***Ribbon In The Sky***
B:***Black Orchid***
US Motown T – 1639F
Songwriter:A:Wonder; B:Wonder/Wright
Producer:Wonder
Released:September 1982 (US)

A:***Front Line***

B:***(Instrumental)***
UK Motown TMG 1289
Songwriter:Wonder
Producer:Wonder
Released:January 1983 (UK)

A:***Happy Birthday***
B:***Extracts From The Speeches Of Dr Martin Luther King***
US Motown M – 4517MG; UK Motown
TMGT 1326
Songwriter:Wonder
Producer:Wonder
Released:November 1983 (US); December
1983 (UK)

A:***I Just Called To Say I Love You***
B:***(Instrumental)***
US Motown 1745MF; UK Motown TMG 1349
Songwriter:Wonder
Producer:Wonder
Released:September 1984 (US); August
1984 (UK)
Reached number 1 US Pop charts; number 1
US R & B charts; number 1 UK charts

A:***Love Light In Flight***
B:***It's More Than You***
UK Motown TMG 1364
Songwriter:A:Wonder; B:Bridges
Producer:Wonder
Released:November 1984 (UK)

A:***Part Time Lover***

B:***(Instrumental)***
US 1808TF; UK ZB 40351
Songwriter:Wonder
Producer:Wonder
Released:August 1985 (US); September
1985 (UK)
Reached number 1 US Pop charts; number 1
US R & B charts

A:***Overjoyed***
B:***(Instrumental)***
US 1832TF; UK ZB 40567M
Songwriter:Wonder
Producer:Wonder
Released:January 1986 (US); February
1986 (UK)

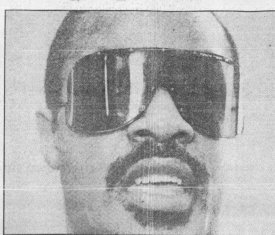

Stevie Wonder is the only black superstar to have supported a variety of political causes. He talks to Robin Denselow about music as a social force

Campaign Wonder

THE London hotel room was set up like a recording studio with banks of keyboards and synthesisers perched on table tops. Seated between them, his head swaying from side to side as he played, was one of the few true living legends of pop music. Stevie Wonder was back in town this week, and as always he brought his music with him.

He may still be only 35, but he has been recording hits for over 20 years this first. Fingertips, was in 1963). Over that period he has established a reputation not just as the greatest black artist in America, but one of the first black artists to appeal to the mass of white rock audiences, to play with the likes of Lennon and Dylan, and consistently use his songs as a means of social comment.

At home in Los Angeles he now owns his own radio station, KJLH, but he insists on behaving agreeably unlike a businessman or a rock star. He was mostly thoughtful and quietly-spoken during the interview (except when he began to mimic others), and then acted like a man obsessed.

He programmed the equipment as if his blindness was no disability to him at all, and an easy, gently stirring riff that he had already written came through the speakers. Over the top of it he began to improvise a melody line, repeating it over and over again. He was already late for a radio interview, but no one disturbed him. He kept playing for over 10 minutes, and it was a rare privilege just to be in the same little room.

Stevie had arrived just a few hours earlier, after being delayed by a broken-down Concorde that carried all this equipment across the Atlantic. He wasn't sure if he was going to record over here (though he might finish off a new song he has written for the young black British singer Junior), but he wanted to explain why his latest album, In Square Circle, had been such a long time in the making.

It's been five years since his last release, Hotter Than July (if one doesn't count the songs he provided for the film The Woman In Red), and even by superstar standards that's slow going. It didn't seem to worry him. "If you are creating, and you have a concept in mind, you have to wait until you are satisfied. The bottom line is to give the best you can."

In Square Circle was originally planned as a double album, but came out as a single "because a double wasn't economically feasible." Even so, the new LP, with its mixture of pop hits like Part-time Lover, and the anti-apartheid protest, It's Wrong, is going to be the first of a three-part series, and In Square Circle 2 should be out next year.

The idea, he said is that the series should deal with experiences people go through in their lives. "The album sleeve is square and the record is round, the earth is round and divided into squares, and we start life at square one and move through the spiral of life, just as you find in a record's grooves."

It's a measure of his genius that at some times his work is private and highly imaginative, but at others it is firmly grounded in reality. Inner Vision contain Stevie's first great self-written social comment song, Living For The City and on almost every album since he has matched the tuneful love songs and ballads, and the hi-tech synthesised dance songs, with an element of social concern.

He is also the only black superstar to have constantly supported a whole variety of causes. In 1971 he appeared with John Lennon at a rally demanding the release of White Panther leader John Sinclair, who has been gaoled for possessing marijuana. It was a somewhat surprising appearance. "I wouldn't say everybody smokes grass, but I think alcohol has killed more people," he says.

Five years later he appeared with Dylan in a benefit for gaoled boxer Hurricane Carter, and in 1980, with the song Happy Birthday, he added his voice to those demanding that the birthday of Martin Luther King be made a national holiday.

Largely because of that song, and the Wonder-inspired campaign that went with it, the request has now been granted. There will be a new American national holiday from next year on,

but it will be on January 20, five days after King's actual birthday. Stevie said he wasn't surprised at his success, "because I just knew that the thrust of energy was there. The naming gives people a chance to examine the principles of Dr King, and understands that these principles are not for one group but for everyone to live by."

On the latest album, Stevie's concern is with apartheid, but he says its just chance that It's Wrong should appear this year. The song was started three years ago, but only recently did he acquire the technology to record it the way he wanted, "sampling" African sounds and programming them into his synthesisers. The music is in his mind, but his actions are still practical. In February this year he was arrested in an anti-apartheid demonstration in Washington. "They said I was disturbing the peace. I was singing."

During '85 other artists have caught up with Stevie in rediscovering music as a social force. He explained it, in a typically unexpected way, like this. "Music has always been a very significant social force. It's value that people put upon it at various times that made it insignificant in their minds. Like sometimes, when you're sleepy, and you're getting home at six in the morning, and you hear the birds singing, you say 'damn – I wish these birds would shut up'. But if you've had great sleep and you hear the birds you say 'wow it's time to get up'. So it's the value we place on it that makes it significant but it really remains the same."

His own heroes include the great black and white artists he has known, and performed with over the past two decades. He enthused about Marvin Gaye's 1972 album What's Going On ("it will be a long time before someone does something to surpass that work, but no, it wasn't the influence for Living For The City").

Asked about Lennon he said he was concerned at the current McCartney versus Lennon controversy. He didn't like gossip, and added, "I wouldn't be a good writer, I'd be boring." He had known Lennon and talked to him a little. "I feel I know him very well through his music. Many people are more expressive in their art than they are when they are talking one to one." After the interview, Stevie Wonder headed straight back to his keyboards.

Stevie Wonder ; picture by Graham Turner

Wonder)/*Yester-Me, Yester-You, Yesterday* (Miller, Wells)/*Angie Girl* (Cosby, Moy, Wonder)/*Give Your Love* (Hunter, Wonder, Cosby)/*I've Got You* (Wonder, Moy)
Produced by Henry Cosby

"Stevie Wonder (Live)"
US Tamla 298; UK Tamla Motown
STML 11150
Released March 1970 (US); June 1970 (UK)
1: *For Once In My Life* (Miller, Murden)/*Pretty World* (Adolfo, Gasper, A & M Bergman)/*Sunny* (Hebb)/*Love Theme From Romeo And Juliet (A Time For Us)* (Kusik, Snyder, Rota)/*Shoo-Be-Doo-Be-Doo-Da-Day* (Cosby, Moy, Wonder)/*Everybody's Talkin'* (Neil)/*My Cherie Amour* (Cosby, Wonder, Moy)/*Yester-Me, Yester-You, Yesterday* (Miller, Wells)/*I've Gotta Be Me* (Marks)/*Once In A Lifetime* (Bricusse, Newley)
2: *A Place In The Sun* (Miller, Wells)/*Down To Earth* (Miller, O'Malley, Vandenberg)/*Blowin' In The Wind* (Dylan)/*By The Time I Get To Phoenix* (Webb)/*Ca 'Purange* (Mussapere)/*Alfie* (Bacharach, David)/*For Once In My Life* (Miller, Murden)/*Thank You Love* (Wonder, Cosby, Moy)
Produced by Henry Cosby and Clarence Paul

"Signed, Sealed And Delivered"
US Tamla 304; UK Tamla Motown
STML 11169
Released August 1970 (US); December 1970 (UK)
1: *Never Had A Dream Come True* (Moy, Wonder, Cosby)/*We Can Work It Out* (Lennon, McCartney)/*Signed, Sealed, Delivered (I'm Yours)* (Wonder, Garrett, Wright, Hardaway)/*Heaven Help Us All* (Miller)/*You Can't Judge A Book By Its Cover* (Wonder, Cosby, Moy)/*Sugar* (Hunter, Wonder)
2: *Don't Wonder Why* (Caston)/*Anything You Want Me To Do* (Hunter, Wonder, Hardaway, Riser)/*I Can't Let My Heaven Walk Away* (Sawyer, Hinton)/*Joy (Takes Me Over)* (Browner)/*I Gotta Have A Song* (Hunter, Wonder, Hardaway, Riser)/*Something To Say* (Hunter, Wonder)
Produced by Stevie Wonder

"Where I'm Coming From"
US Tamla 308; UK Tamla Motown
STML 11183
Released April 1971 (US); June 1971 (UK)
1: *Look Around* (Wright, Wonder)/*Do Yourself A Favour* (Wright, Wonder)/*Think Of Me As Your Soldier* (Wright, Wonder)/*Something Out Of The Blue* (Wonder, Wright)/*If You Really Love Me* (Wonder, Wright)

2: *I Wanna Talk To You* (Wonder, Wright)/*Take Up A Course In Happiness* (Wonder, Wright)/*Never Dreamed You'd Leave In Summer* (Wonder, Wright)/*Sunshine In Your Eyes* (Wonder, Wright)
Produced by Stevie Wonder

"Stevie Wonder's Greatest Hits Vol. 2"
US Tamla 313; UK Tamla Motown
STML 11196
Released 1971 (US); February 1972 (UK)
1: *Shoo-Be-Doo-Be-Doo-Da-Day* (Moy, Cosby, Wonder)/*Signed, Sealed, Delivered*

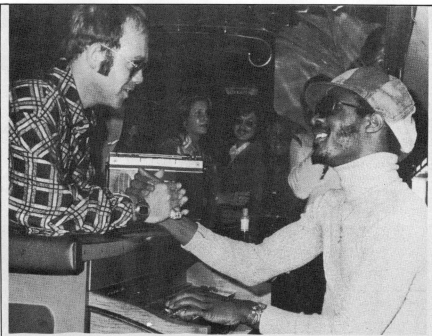

WHAT A WONDER!—Elton John was surprised when he discovered that Stevie Wonder was a surprise guest on the "Starship Jet" that is carrying John and his band across America on their 1973 tour. Stevie, in his first public appearance since his near fatal accident in North Carolina several weeks ago, greeted Elton with a medley of Elton John hits aboard the plane which landed in Boston for a concert at the Boston Gardens. Wonder and Elton performed "Honky Tonky Women" together at the concert.
Stevie and Elton are both presently in the charts. Wonder's "Innervisions" on Motown and John with "Goodbye Yellow Brick Road" on MCA.

(I'm Yours) (Hardaway, Wright, Wonder, Garrett)/*If You Really Love Me* (Wright, Wonder)/*For Once In My Life* (Miller, Murden)/*We Can Work It Out* (Lennon, McCartney)/*You Met Your Match* (Wonder, Hunter, Hardaway)
2: *Never Had A Dream Come True* (Wonder, Moy, Cosby)/*Yester-Me, Yester-You, Yesterday* (Miller, Wells)/*My Cherie Amour* (Wonder, Moy, Cosby)/*Never Dreamed You'd Leave In Summer* (Wonder, Wright)/*Travelin' Man* (Miller, Wells)/*Heaven Help Us All* (Miller)
The UK version has different track listings
Various producers

"Music Of My Mind"
US Tamla 314; UK Tamla Motown STMA 8002
Released March 1972 (US), May 1972 (UK)
1: *Love Having You Around* (Wonder,

Wright)/*Superwoman* (Wonder)/*I Love Everything About You* (Wonder)/*Sweet Little Girl* (Wonder)
2: *Happier Than The Morning Sun* (Wonder)/*Girl Blue* (Wonder, Wright)/*Seems So Long* (Wonder)/*Keep On Running* (Wonder)/*Evil* (Wonder, Wright)
Produced by Stevie Wonder

"Talking Book"
US Tamla 319; UK Tamla Motown STMA 8007
Released 1972 (US); January 1973 (UK)
1: *You Are The Sunshine Of My Life* (Wonder)/*Maybe Your Baby* (Wonder)/*You And I* (Wonder)/*Tuesday Heartbreak* (Wonder)/*You've Got It Bad Girl* (Wright)
2: *Superstition* (Wonder)/*Big Brother* (Wonder)/*Blame It On The Sun* (Wonder, Wright)/*Looking For Another Pure Love* (Wonder)/*I Believe (When I Fall In Love It

Will Be Forever) (Wonder, Wright)
Produced by Stevie Wonder

"Inner Visions"
US Tamla 326; UK Tamla Motown STMA 8011
Released August 1973 (US); October 1973 (UK)
1: *Too High* (Wonder)/*Visions* (Wonder)/*Living For The City* (Wonder)/*Golden Lady* (Wonder)
2: *Higher Ground* (Wonder)/*Jesus Children Of America* (Wonder)/*All In Love Is Fair* (Wonder)/*Don't You Worry 'Bout A Thing* (Wonder)/*He's Misstra Know-It-All* (Wonder)
Produced by Stevie Wonder

"Fulfillingness' First Finale"
US Tamla 332; UK Tamla Motown STMA 8019
Released July 1974 (US); September 1974 (UK)
1: *Smile Please* (Wonder)/*Heaven Is 10 Zillion Light Years Away* (Wonder)/*Too Shy To Say* (Wonder)/*Boogie On Reggae Woman* (Wonder)/*Creepin'* (Wonder)
2: *You Haven't Done Nothin'* (Wonder)/*It Ain't No Use* (Wonder)/*They Won't Go When I Go* (Wonder, Wright)/*Bird Of Beauty* (Wonder)/*Please Don't Go* (Wonder)
Produced by Stevie Wonder

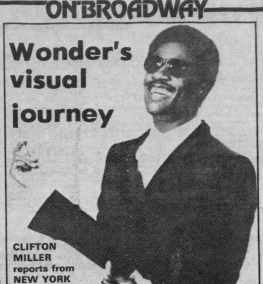

Wonder's visual journey

On the road with Wonderlove and the 45-piece National Afro-American Orchestra, Stevie has been showcasing virtually the entire contents of his 'Journey Through The Secret Life Of Plants' album.

It's a shrewd move, for the two-disk set has been criticized here as too self-indulgent, too lacking in fresh ideas.

Seeing Stevie perform the music live lends it more perspective, makes it more accessible, and re-emphasizes — as only in-person appearances can do — his sensitivity, his humor, his exuberance.

The concerts were also designed to add some visual images to Stevie's 'Plants' work, in the absence of the movie for which he originally wrote the score (though there's now some word that the film might be released by Paramount in the New Year, after it's launched 'Star Trek').

The Wonder show opens with the Afro-American Orchestra playing the opening theme from 'Plants', entitled 'Earth's Creation,' while the opening footage from the flick is visible on backscreen projection.

Then, from somewhere backstage, Stevie's harmonica motif in 'The First Garden' is audible, becoming louder as he's led on to his stage-centre battery of keyboards: Piano, Synthesizer, Clavinet.

From there, he takes the audience through their 'Journey' via 'Voyage To India,' 'Same Old Story,' 'Venus' Flytrap And The Bug,' 'Seasons,' 'Power Flower,' 'Send One Your Love,' 'Race Babbling,' 'Outside My Window,' 'Black

CLIFTON MILLER reports from NEW YORK

STEVE WONDER: a trip down Memory Lane...

Orchid,' 'Come Back As A Flower' and 'A Seed's A Star & Tree Medley,' in fine style.

The show's second half starts with a marvellous step back in time, as Wonderlove cranks up into the 'Fingertips' riff, an MC announces 'Ladies and gentlemen, it's . . . Little Stevie Wonder,'' and Stevie is led on, wearing vintage '63 dark glasses and over-sized suit.

He then proceeds to deliver a full-length version of 'Fingertips,' his first major hit, complete with call-and-response from the audience as

on the original recording.

With the band still playing, Stevie's then led offstage, still bopping around as he must have done a million times in the early Sixties Motortown Revues.

It's a stunning piece of nostalgia, a tribute to the past handled with more class and affection than any other Motown star has managed, in this reporter's experience.

After a minute or so, Stevie returns as the man, the mature musician, and moves into an action-packed, 90-minute showcase of hits old

and new, including 'Signed, Sealed, Delivered,' 'Never Dreamed You'd Leave In Summer,' 'My Cherie Amour,' 'For Once In My Life,' 'Superwoman,' 'Boogie On Reggae Woman,' 'Living For The City,' 'Superstition,' 'Don't You Worry 'Bout A Thing,' 'I Wish,' 'Sir Duke' and more.

The concert concludes with the finale of 'The Secret Life Of Plants,' with the National Afro-American Orchestra back on stage to support Stevie through the

LP's striking title song, a climactic and well-considered consummation of Wonder's first U.S. concert dates in five years — and testimony to the man's colossal and continuing talent.

* * *

STEVIE WONDER was also on national television here in early December, as one of three guests on a special hosted by Barbara Walters.

Walters, a former TV news announcer turned "personality" journalist, is the master of the banal question, the foolish enquiry — made all the worse by the fact that she lisps.

"Did you have to be born blind," she asks Stevie for openers, following up with such stunners as "Do you ever feel sorry for yourself," and so on.

But there was one interesting moment, when Walters recalled what Wonder said earlier this year, at the funeral of Berry Gordy's father.

"I used to feel that by 1980, or the end of it, my life would no longer be," she quotes him as saying then. Then she enquires: "What did you mean by that, why did you think you weren't going to live to be older?"

Replied Stevie, "Well, I will not completely get into it, but I will say that there is a belief that I have, and that belief is not to make one feel sad; that is a belief that is a feeling that I accept."

Continued Walters: "Is something going to happen to you? Do you think you're going to get sick; do you think you might take your own life?"

"Never gonna take my own life," swiftly responded Stevie.

"Then why," said Walters, "do you think your life is going to be short?"

Concluded Stevie, enigmatically, "It's a feeling, OK? And if feelings don't lie, then it's so."

Yesterday (Miller, Wells)/*Never Had A Dream Come True* (Wonder, Moy, Cosby)/*Signed, Sealed, Delivered, (I'm Yours)* (Wonder, Wright, Garrett, Hardaway)
6: *Heaven Help Us All* (Miller)/*I Gotta Have A Song* (Wonder, Hunter, Hardaway, Riser)/*Never Dreamed You'd Leave In Summer* (Wonder, Wright)/*If You Really Love Me* (Wonder, Wright)/*Something Out Of The Blue* (Wonder, Wright)/*Do Yourself A Favour* (Wonder, Wright)
Various producers

"Stevie Wonder's Journey Through The Secret Life Of Plants" (Double)
US Tamla 371; UK Motown TMSP 6009
Released October 1979 (US and UK)
1: *Earth's Creation* (Wonder)/*The First Garden* (Wonder)/*Voyage To India* (Wonder)/*Same Old Story* (Wonder)/*Venus' Flytrap And The Bug* (Wonder)/*Ai No Sono* (Wonder)
2: *Seasons* (Wonder)/*Flower Power* (Wonder, Sembello)/*Send One Your Love (instrumental)* (Wonder)/*Race Babbling* (Wonder)
3: *Send One Your Love* (Wonder)/*Outside My Window* (Wonder)/*Black Orchid* (Wonder, Wright)/*Ecclesiastes* (Wonder)/*Kesse Ye Lolo De Ye* (Wonder)/

"Songs In The Key Of Life" (Double)
US Tamla 340; UK Motown TMSP 6002
Released September 1976 (US); November 1976 (UK)
1: *Love's In Need Of Love Today* (Wonder)/*Have A Talk With God* (Wonder, Hardaway)/*Village Ghetto Land* (Wonder, Byrd)/*Contusion* (Wonder)/*Sir Duke* (Wonder)
2: *I Wish* (Wonder)/*Knocks Me Off My Feet* (Wonder)/*Pastime Paradise* (Wonder)/*Summer Soft* (Wonder)/*Ordinary Pain* (Wonder)
3: *Isn't She Lovely* (Wonder)/*Joy Inside My Tears* (Wonder)/*Black Man* (Wonder)
4: *Ngiculela-Es Una Historia – I Am Singing* (Wonder)/*If It's Magic* (Wonder)/*As* (Wonder)/*Another Star* (Wonder)
Produced by Stevie Wonder

"A Something's Extra Bonus Record" (EP)
1: *Saturn* (Wonder, Sembello)/*Ebony Eyes* (Wonder)
2: *All Day Sucker* (Wonder)/*Easy Goin' Evening (My Mama's Call)* (Wonder)

"Looking Back" (known as "Anthology") (Triple)
US Motown M9 804; UK Motown M9 804
Released December 1977 (US and UK)
1: *Thank You (For Loving Me All The Way)* (Paul, Holland, Stevenson)/*Contract On

Love* (Bradford, Dozier, Holland)/*Fingertips (Part 2)* (Cosby, Paul)/*Workout, Stevie, Workout* (Paul, Cosby)/*Castles In The Sand* (Davis, Gordon, Wilson, O'Brien)/*Hey Harmonica Man* (Cooper, Josie)/*High Heel Sneakers* (Higgenbotham)
2: *Uptight (Everything's Alright)* (Moy, Wonder, Cosby)/*Nothing's Too Good For My Baby* (Moy, Cosby, Stevenson)/*Blowin' In The Wind* (Dylan)/*Ain't That Asking For Trouble* (Moy, Wonder, Paul)/*I'd Cry* (Wonder, Moy)/*A Place In The Sun* (Miller, Wells)/*Sylvia* (Wonder, Moy, Cosby)
3: *Down To Earth* (Miller, O'Malley, Vandenberg)/*Thank You Love* (Wonder, Moy, Cosby)/*Hey Love* (Wonder, Paul, Broadnax)/*Travelin' Man* (Miller, Wells)/*Until You Come Back To Me (That's What I'm Gonna Do)* (Wonder, Paul, Broadnax)/*I Was Made To Love Her* (Wonder, Cosby, Moy, Hardaway)/*I'm Wondering* (Moy, Wonder, Cosby)
4: *Shoo-Be-Doo-Be-Doo-Da-Day* (Wonder, Cosby, Moy)/*You Met Your Match* (Wonder, Hunter, Hardaway)/*I'd Be A Fool Right Now* (Wonder, Moy, Cosby)/*Alfie* (Bacharach, David)/*More Than A Dream* (Wonder, Cosby)/*For Once In My Life* (Miller, Murden)
5: *Angie Girl* (Wonder, Moy, Cosby)/*My Cherie Amour* (Wonder, Moy, Cosby)/*Don't Know Why I Love You* (Wonder, Hunter, Riser, Hardaway)/*If I Ruled The World* (Bricusse, Ornadel)/*Yester-Me, Yester-You,

Stevie Wonder and 'the Clock of Now'

By Robert Hilburn
Los Angeles Times Service

LOS ANGELES — You get an idea of how hard Stevie Wonder works on his music when you listen to him describe the thought he puts into selecting his album titles. Rather than naming the album after one of the collection's most appealing songs, Wonder wants his titles to represent the direction and tone of his records.

Wonder, 35, said "In Square Circle" was chosen as the title of his newly released album to suggest the complexities and ironies of human experience.

"Take the album itself — the cover is square, but the record itself is a circle," he said. "But also the world is round even though it is based off in squares — with north, east, south and west. In the West, most buildings are built in the square form, but a lot of the African buildings of old are built in the circular form.

"There is also the need to pay careful attention to things because they often are not what they seem. Some of the songs talk about this. You have many people these days who try to convince you that they are acting in God's name — as if he okays what they are doing. But they are actually just using the creator's name to justify their own selfish motives.

"Take the apartheid song on the album. That's a perfect example of a government that says it acts in God's name."

The song — "It's Wrong (Apartheid)" — speaks to rulers and oppressed blacks in South Africa. The album version of the song ends with an expression of hope to the latter: "Freedom is coming... hold on tight."

The song will be extended on the still-unreleased 12-inch single and on the compact-disc version of the album to include this warning to South African officials:

The clock of now says it's time
For you to make up your mind
Before it's too late for you
To earn your redemption.

Wonder has had a steady series of hits in recent years, including "Master Blaster (Jammin')" in 1980 and "That Girl" in 1982, and he won an Academy Award for "I Just Called to Say I Love You" from the film "The Woman in Red."

Still, he maintained something of a low profile in the 1980s after establishing himself in the 1970s as one of the most gifted and acclaimed figures of modern pop. His dominance was highlighted in the mid-1970s when three consecutive Wonder albums won best-album Grammys: "Innervisions," "Fulfillingness' First Finale" and "Songs in the Key of Life."

Although the album that followed, the sound track for the documentary "Journey Through the Secret Life of Plants," was an exquisite musical statement, its esoteric de-

Stevie Wonder: "Freedom is coming... hold on tight."

sign was not what the public or the industry was expecting, and it was widely viewed as a disappointment. Still, the two-record set is likely to stand as one of Wonder's top achievements.

While the follow-up, "Hotter Than July," was generally admired and sold well, it did not catch the pop imagination the way his earlier work had. The sound track to Gene Wilder's comedy "The Woman in Red" was a mostly light-hearted sidestep.

Wonder sees the new album as the start of his most ambitious series of albums since the 1970s trilogy. "This is the first of a group of three albums," he said. "Some of the songs will deal with relationships and love, some with political themes and social issues, and some just with religious beliefs and concepts."

There is an exuberance and grace to the best songs in the new album that echo the ambition and confidence of the early work.

Wonder, a participant in the "We Are the World" recording session for African famine aid, is one of many artists who are helping restore a sense of social consciousness to pop.

Unlike some of them, however, he is no newcomer to social commentary, although his importance as a commentator in pop is often overlooked because he puts his thoughts into such a melodic and accessible format.

A classic example was "You Haven't Done Nothin'," one of the most scathing attacks of the 1970s on governmental indifference to-

ward the disadvantaged — backed by a vigorous, danceable tune. Other songs touched on such matters as the difficulty of Vietnam veterans in readjusting to life at home; one song called for a national holiday in memory of Martin Luther King.

Because of that number, "Happy Birthday," Wonder was associated with the drive to honor the memory of King, and he was thrilled when Congress voted to establish the third Monday in January, effective next year, as a national holiday. (King's birthday was Jan 15.) Wonder was in the U.S. Senate gallery with Coretta King, the widow of the slain civil rights leader, and her son on the day in 1983 that the bill passed.

Wonder is encouraged by the upswing of social awareness and responsibility among pop artists.

"I think it took a long time for people to get over the disillusionment of losing such very great people," he said, referring to the assassinations of King and John F. Kennedy.

The memory of the 1960s, Wonder said, had somewhat faded until recently. "The younger generation, black and white, didn't know a lot about the struggle that had gone on," he said. "They took for granted a lot of the advances that were made.

"That may be why so many young people today have such a conservative attitude. The interesting thing is that a lot of the momentum for this renewal is coming from people my age, people who grew up in the '60s and did see what happened. A lot of these people realize it is time to get involved again."

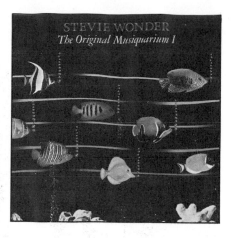

4: *I Wish* (Wonder)/*Isn't She Lovely* (Wonder)/*Do I Do* (Wonder)
Produced by Stevie Wonder

"The Woman In Red" (Selections From The Original Motion Picture Soundtrack)
US Motown 6108 ML; UK Motown ZL 72285
Released August 1984 (US); September 1984 (UK)
1: *The Woman In Red* (Wonder)/*It's You* (with Dionne Warwick) (Wonder)/*It's More Than You* (Bridges)/*I Just Called To Say I Love You* (Wonder)
2: *Love Light In Flight* (Wonder)/*Moments Aren't Moments* (vocal by Dionne Warwick) (Wonder)/*Weakness* (with Dionne Warwick) (Wonder)/*Don't Drive Drunk* (Wonder)
Produced by Stevie Wonder

"In Square Circle"
US Tamla 6134 TL; UK ZL 72005
Released September 1985 (US and UK)
1: *Part Time Lover* (Wonder)/*I Love You Too Much* (Wonder)/*Whereabouts* (Wonder)/*Stranger On The Shore Of Love* (Wonder)/*Never In Your Sun* (Wonder)
2: *Spiritual Walkers* (Wonder)/*Land Of La La* (Wonder)/*Go Home* (Wonder)/*Overjoyed* (Wonder)/*It's Wrong (Apartheid)* (Wonder)
Produced by Stevie Wonder and Gary Olazaba

Come Back As A Flower (Wonder, Wright)
4: *A Seed's A Star/Tree Medley* (Wonder, Andrews)/*The Secret Life Of Plants* (Wonder)/*Tree* (Wonder)/*Finale* (Wonder)
Produced by Stevie Wonder.

"Hotter Than July"
US Tamla 373; UK Motown STMA 8035
Released October 1980 (US); November 1980 (UK)
1: *Did I Hear You Say You Love Me?* (Wonder)/*All I Do* (Wonder)/*Rocket Love* (Wonder)/*I Ain't Gonna Stand For It* (Wonder)/*As If You Read My Mind* (Wonder)
2: *Masterblaster (Jammin')* (Wonder)/*Do Like You* (Wonder)/*Cash In Your Face* (Wonder)/*Lately* (Wonder)/*Happy Birthday* (Wonder)

Produced by Stevie Wonder

"Stevie Wonder's Original Musiquarium 1" (Double)
US Tamla 6002 TL2; UK Motown TMSP 6012
Released May 1982 (US); July 1982 (UK)
1: *Superstition* (Wonder)/*You Haven't Done Nothin'* (Wonder)/*Living For The City* (Wonder)/*Front Line* (Wonder)
2: *Superwoman (Where Were You When I Needed You)* (Wonder)/*Send One Your Love* (Wonder)/*You Are The Sunshine Of My Life* (Wonder)/*Ribbon In The Sky* (Wonder)
3: *Higher Ground* (Wonder)/*Sir Duke* (Wonder)/*Masterblaster (Jammin')* (Wonder)/*Boogie On Reggae Woman* (Wonder)/*That Girl* (Wonder)

Acknowledgments

A number of people helped in various ways to see this book through to its completion. Sharon Gude provided invaluable help with research both original and secondary, and Gilbert Gude helped by supplying historical details and access to the many books I consulted at the Library of Congress. Fred Goodman and Frank Spotnitz were generous in supplying invaluable unpublished interviews with Stevie Wonder. Harry Weinger offered encouragement, editorial advice and his dauntless enthusiasm for Stevie Wonder at a crucial point. Thanks to Ed for answering phones, Barbara Mathe for editing and encouragement, Bob Rankin for the ride through Letchworth Park, Michael Neve, Justin Pearson and Reg Venters. Jane Friedman of Wartoke Concern Inc., who handled Stevie Wonder's public relations throughout the seventies, offered valuable insight and access to her files as well as supplying many of the photographs reproduced in this book.

Other source material used in preparing this book includes the *New York Times*, *Washington Post*, *Newsweek*, *Rolling Stone*, *Esquire*, *New Musical Express*, *Jet*, *Ebony*, *People*, *Crawdaddy*, the *Village Voice*, the *Baltimore Evening Sun*, *Stereo Review*, *Soul Teen*, *Downbeat*, *Rock World*, *Melody Maker*, *Exit*, the *Birmingham Times* (US), the *Honolulu Advertiser*, *Disc*, *Viva*, *Gallery*, the *Afro-American*, the *Guardian*, *Los Angeles Times* and the *International Herald Tribune*.

For their help and support visually, I would like to thank Ken Kitchen for designing the book and conceptualizing the cover design from a photograph by David Redfern and creative artwork by Richard Manning. The following individuals, collectors, picture agencies and record companies all contributed to the gathering of photographs for this book and I would like to extend my special gratitude to them: Tony Reilly of Motown Records, Veronica Jones of Motown Records, Black Bull Presentations Inc., Paul Slade/ Pictorial Parade, Syndication International, S & G Press Agency, London Features International, Kwame Braithwaite, Wide World Pictures Inc., Topham Picture Library, Retna Pictures Limited, Associated Press, Michael Ochs Archive, Barry Plummer, Chuck Pulin, *Black Echoes*, *Blues and Soul*, Charlie Gillett/BMI Music, Pictorial Press, Tom Sheehan, John McKenzie/PPS, Wartoke Concern Inc., Harry Goodwin, Kate Simon, Justin Thomas, William Eastabrook, John Bardazzi, Jeffrey Mayer, Frank Dandridge, Iain Dickson, Sharon Davis and Roger St Pierre. Special thanks to Linda McCartney for her photograph on page 129. It has not always been possible to trace the copyright sources, and the publisher would be glad to hear from any such unacknowledged copyright holders.

I would like to thank John Brown, Peter Hogan and Pete Townshend of Eel Pie for supporting the original idea and my editor and publisher Sandra Wake whose encouragement and enthusiasm carried the project through.

Finally, from one Taurean to another, thanks Stevie and nice to have met you.

John Swenson